VIRTUAL SELLING

✳✳✳

By

Matt Goldemb

Goldemb© Copyright 2020

All Rights Reserved.

This report aims to provide precise and robust information on the issue and issue secured. The output could be rendered with the prospect of the manufacturer not needing to do bookkeeping, officially licensed or otherwise eligible administrations. Should an exhortation be relevant, lawful, or qualified, a rehearsed individual in the call should be required.

The Statement of Principles approved and endorsed by the American Bar Association Committee and the Publications and Associations Commission.

It is not lawful to reproduce, copy, or distribute any portion of this study using either electronic methods or the community written. The registering of this delivery is deliberately disallowed, with the exception of written distributor authorization, the ability of this material is not permitted. All resources are retained.

The information provided is conveyed to be truthful and consistent, in so far as any chance, in the absence of thinking or something else, of any usage or misuse of any methods, procedures, or cookies found within is the special and definite responsibility of the receiver peruser. Any civil duty or liability shall be put upon the seller for any reparation, damage, or money-related misfortune attributable to the data received, whether explicitly or indirectly.

Those authors assert all copyrights which the seller does not retain.

The statistics herein are solely for instructional purposes and are all-. The details were reached without consent or acknowledgment of guarantee.

The markings used shall be without permission, and without the approval or the help of the proprietor of the label shall be published. All logos and trademarks in this book are for information purposes only and are held explicitly by individuals who are not affiliated with this document.

Table of Contents

A BRIEF INTRODUCTION ON THE WORLD OF VIRTUAL SELLING . 6

VIRTUAL SALES: A NEW ERA IS AROUND THE CORNER 12

WHAT DOES VIRTUAL SELLING MEAN FOR YOUR SELLERS "IN THE FIELD." 19

SPEAK AN EXPERT: HOW TO SWITCH TO VIRTUAL SALES TO HELP YOUR COMPANY SURVIVE COVID-19 28

DIGITAL ERA SALES: WHY EVERY SALES PROFESSIONAL MUST UNDERSTAND DIGITAL MARKETING 37

    REACH CUSTOMER ATTENTION THROUGH DIGITAL TRANSFORMATION 52

VIRTUAL SALES SERVICES 64

    HOW TO GET ONLINE PURCHASES IN 6 SIMPLE MEASURES .. 64

    THE MINIMUM REQUIREMENTS TO CREATE A COMMERCIAL ACTIVITY 73

    DIGITAL TRANSFORMATION: FREE DIGITAL TRANSFORMATION GUIDE 80

    TECHNICAL EQUIPMENT: WEBSITE, APP AND VIRTUAL PLATFORMS 116

    INCREDIBLE TECHNICAL TOOLS FOR BEST VIRTUAL MEETINGS 137

    CASCADING EFFECTS OF VIRTUAL SALES ON SALES OPERATIONS 154

BUILD THE MARKETING LANDSCAPE 157

WHAT IS CUSTOMER CENTRICITY IN A DIGITAL WORLD? 189

    THE FIVE BEST WAYS TO RECEIVE CUSTOMER FEEDBACK ... 193

DESCRIPTIONS OF IDEAL PEOPLE PARTICIPATING IN VIRTUAL SALES 208

THE SELLER'S GUIDE: SUCCESSFUL ADVICE IN A VIRTUAL SALES WORLD..220

MINDSET AND MOTIVATION 229

SEVEN-TIME MANAGEMENT TIPS NEEDED FOR SALES REPS...233

COOPERATION WITH BUYERS 238

EFFECTIVE VIRTUAL NEGOTIATION 246

WHAT IS BRAND IDENTITY? 251

CONCLUSION..266

A BRIEF INTRODUCTION ON THE WORLD OF VIRTUAL SELLING

Virtual Selling

Empower Your Sales Team to Sell Virtually

Our current operating environment requires a change in the way we interact and sell to customers. We no longer have the advantage of meeting and connecting in-person - options that we may have taken for granted in developing relationships and trust.

The way we have prepared, implemented, and followed customer dialogues and sales opportunities must adapt. Sales professionals need to overcome the artificial barrier that exists when selling in a virtual environment by using their sales skills to retain, customize, and disarm customers.

Virtual selling requires a significant change in traditional sales skills to create a more engaging and connected shopping experience.

For remote distribution situations, people act differently. They're not the same and are easier to divert from each other. Video sale's superficial and often casual nature causes a difference in conventional ways of sales based on formality and the real interactions that people experience as they sit down.

There are many pitfalls during virtual sales meetings. To avoid these pitfalls, it is necessary to use sales skills and techniques, which must be carried out with a greater sense of intentionality.

The willingness of a seller to appear credible on the video, establish a real connection, and engage in meaningful interactions that create trust is fundamental. Small mistakes mean more distractions.

Richardson Sales Performance's new virtual sales training program provides sales representatives with the skills and techniques to increase credibility, connect, promote openness, and build confidence in virtual sales meetings to boost and gain sales opportunities.

The program includes:

- Preparation: distance selling requires a higher level of preparation for managing the environment. Professionalism and credibility of the project; Building a relationship, using technology effectively, Set expectations for the camera, and carefully create materials that improve and support commitment without distracting from a real conversation.
- Virtual sales skills: sales skills must be of a higher level to show virtual presence and engage in meaningful discussions while keeping the customer's attention.
- Meeting structure and moderation skills: Increase beneficial outcomes by developing a specifically defined group whiteboard and using mediation methods in a simulated world to control resources and stakeholders.

It is more difficult to sell in a virtual world than to sell face-to-face, particularly when selling people are forced to hold an online sales meeting with little experience or preparation.

Sales managers need to create calm and confident so that sellers can focus on the right things.

Sellers must offer customers peace of mind and confidence to make their businesses work. To execute a virtual selling campaign in full, dealers need a game plan, health, and ability. Praxis in a simulated world is the best way to develop trust and abilities.

Much as in football, it is the team that typically has the edge and is better prepared. Providing sellers with an understanding of the unique challenges, a range of best practices, and many practices will help sellers continue to converse significantly and build the confidence customers need to make purchasing decisions in these difficult times.

OBJECTIVES OF THE VIRTUAL SALES TRAINING PROGRAM

By learning virtual sales skills, your salespeople can more effectively engage their customers in virtual meetings and conduct training courses to:

- Apply best practices for virtual sales skills to increase credibility, connect, foster openness and build trust remotely to increase momentum and seize opportunities

- Boost meeting results by creating a clear meeting schedule and moderation techniques to manage time and stakeholders in a remote sales meeting
- Use virtual presence to bring energy into the virtual environment and encourage the commitment to replicate the personalized and meaningful interactions that occur most naturally in a personal environment
- Diagnose ways to increase effectiveness by understanding the benefits, challenges, and pitfalls of selling in a virtual environment
- Apply the best virtual preparation practices to maximize professionalism, take advantage of technological tools and create materials that improve and support involvement without distracting from a real conversation

DELIVERY OF THE VIRTUAL SALES PROGRAM

Interactive 4-hour workshop led by a virtual teacher

- Breakout sessions in small groups
- Provides best practices for virtual sales
- Use zoom
- Agnostic methodology
- Can be adjusted within the scope

VIRTUAL SALES: A NEW ERA IS AROUND THE CORNER

Face-to-face sales are over. How can you upgrade your sales organization to sell effectively in this new environment?

The latest developments around the world have intensified the rise in retail sales over the last two decades. Talk of it, even without a global pandemic among humanity. Our universe is where you can go online, buy a car in seconds, and deliver it to your home the next day. The B2B consumers did the same thing in just a matter of days. The field of B2C has grown in the B2B area for some time, with personal sales being just one example.

Before dividing it into a few categories, read the COVID 19 action plan for sales managers. There you can see how we deal with in this blog fits the general picture we have put together to deal with the uncertainty of this current situation. As a quick preview, the first steps are to get in touch with your team and your customers to ensure their physical and mental security in these difficult times.

Focus on Phone and Virtual Sales Enablement

Ok, now that you have seen how this fits the big picture, let's talk about selling in a virtual world through the objective of 5 main categories:

1. Prospecting

We will start with a simple one. This part of face-to-face sales has already become largely virtual. You can no longer be an effective representative if you do not know how to create an insightful LinkedIn message or acquire the first two minutes of a phone call. Cold calls are still very effective for recording. However, it is no longer the "smile and dial" approach from a long list of phone numbers. Organizations become smarter by segmenting and prioritizing their potential customers (and customers) based on potential, thereby aligning the best people with the accounts representing the highest potential revenue. To search in a virtual environment, you need to have a list of priorities that employees can work on. Otherwise, abrasion and productivity decrease significantly.

2. Technology

We are technological agnostics at the SBI. We have seen our customers effectively use all types of CRM software, sales engagement tools, and gamification platforms. A common theme we have seen with customers of all sizes is that technology loses all its value if its structure and processes are damaged. Do you think your team will be more effective if your sales process is not well defined or focused on the customer, and you integrate it into your brand new CRM? It is generally better to have a well defined selling process that is customer-oriented, with no CRM.

3. Representative skills / talents

This new world of virtual sales requires you to change your mind about the skills you consider when you decide to stop selling. The key skills that make an excellent seller remain the same, but some skills will now be more important. For example, becoming a better seller has been proven to be capable of creating relationships. It brings on an entirely different significance in today's modern world. You have fewer chances of engaging with the simulated world and less exposure to the decision-makers that you want to meet. Your teams are in constant competition for Mind Share. If your team is unable to build relationships by sharing interesting insights on LinkedIn or other virtual media, it will never be successful in this new world. Now is the opportunity to look back and assess salespeople's strengths and shortcomings. This should be a quarterly exercise.

4. Demo of a solution

As this post discussed earlier, buyers need a good explanation of what they purchase from B2C. We have found that B2B decision-makers are constantly making buying decisions through their network. How does that mean? What does that mean? This means your success ultimately relies on your ability to test your idea or solution digitally. The related criteria of product and technology are broad and suit your blog best. If the selling staff can't show by themselves without the help of a software expert, you should find the most effective and interactive way to deliver it. It may seem obvious, but your sales teams need to be experts in the products/solutions they sell. This means that you can guide potential customers through a demo of your solution and answer 2nd and 3rd level questions. Nothing makes a potential buyer more than a salesperson who has to repeat over and over again: "I have to get in touch with you about this question." Make sure your employees are constantly trained on the product and offer them the opportunity to succeed.

5. Digital transactions

You may have found a growing topic by now. B2B decision-makers expect more and more B2C services. This means that every single sales manager should consider how to offer a self-service sales movement geared towards their smaller and potential customers. It may sound easy, but it takes tremendous teamwork between advertising, marketing, IT, finance, and legislation to introduce a self-service portal. It also needs a detailed, well defined, and non-corrupted lead routing mechanism and a market distribution model focused on sales potential. You need to ensure that the Self Service Platform is targeted only to the smallest business section. You will have a huge effect on potential wages. Assume that in a big conglomerate, a small team goes to your website and fills out a form to pick "less than 50 employees" because they think about a small "company." When you are running a single lead routing process, and this online form submission is based on your coverage layout and sent to the self-service portal. In this situation, the customer sells the goods and gets profits, but the chances of growth within the big conglomerate have diminished dramatically.

Suppose you have not yet reviewed the COVID 19 sales manager action plan. In that case, we recommend that you go there or bookmark it for later review to make sure you have all the potential current and future implications of this current situation to consider. The five components of virtual sales we talked about above are just a small insight into what to consider. Defining the sales plans and the three-year GTM strategy is quite difficult even at certain times. For all businesses shortly, workplace welfare and support must remain a top priority. It is not too early, though, to talk about how the selling company needs to be built to be competitive in this new climate.

WHAT DOES VIRTUAL SELLING MEAN FOR YOUR SELLERS "IN THE FIELD."

The sale during social distances certainly requires changes for the teams on the field. More than for others, a bigger transition. Any challenges have to be addressed in the near term, but when things return to normal, they are not too early to think of what will happen.

Your sales representatives are certainly not strangers to telephone or web meetings, but until we stay away from CoVid-10, all they can do is resell. Does this mean that the entire sales organization has just switched to an internal sales model? What happens when everything is clarified?

Short-term reality: consider the choices customers face What should customers do with historical purchase patterns that don't fit the stereotype within the sales pattern when their office is locked from home? There are two main options:

Postpone the purchase until you get the usual demo, discussion, or face-to-face meeting. Customers who opted for this option probably initially lacked a convincing event, or the event itself was interrupted as long as the conversation about the office water cooler.

Purchase transition practically because it is critical to the business, and they cannot afford to wait. The calendar is still ongoing, agreements are running out, and some things just need to be addressed if people can get together in an office or not.

If your sales representatives have not already done so, the first activity should be to quickly determine which category each opportunity falls into in their active pipeline. Given market uncertainty, employees naturally place great emphasis on completing the active pipeline rather than building a new one. Quickly identifying opportunities that can still be completed ensures that time is spent where the needle can be moved more in this environment.

Not all "repetitions on the pitch" are the same: this will be a bigger change for some more than others.

We use the term "sales force" to distinguish ourselves from the diversified movement within sales. We do not pretend that sales representatives have never sold on the phone or are unfamiliar with online work. Many already perform most of their duties and reserve personal meetings virtually if the client so wishes, or consider it essential for success. By definition, the short-term change for these sales representatives will not be so drastic that they have already invested in the processes and skills needed to work virtually. Personally.

For sales representatives who are NOT used to virtual sales, the major short-term changes are likely to occur in the sales process's two general stages:

Provide demos, collaborate and participate virtually in more complex discussions

We noted earlier that, given the uncertainty in the corporate environment, most employees would focus on short-term opportunities in flight in their active conduct and not necessarily on pipeline construction. Therefore, the correct execution of the intermediate phase in the advanced stages of the sales process can reveal some gaps in your skills and require training.

Recommended Action: Ensure that teams (including customer-facing SMEs, pre-sales engineers, etc.) have an adequate technological solution to conduct online demonstrations/meetings.

Get buyer's approval by order acceptance/booking guidelines.

If your organization has already invested and introduced an electronic signature feature, this issue is controversial. If this is not the case in your organization, there are several things you can do:

Recommended Measures: Providing a new electronic signature feature takes time. Therefore, the first step should be to review the order acceptance/booking guidelines and understand the impact on employees who can no longer receive a physically signed contract. Secondly, you should work with the law and finances to determine if changes can be made temporarily. For example, if your circumstances are such that law and finance accept the image of an agreement scanned via e-mail based on the circumstances, the policies will need to be updated. The new guidelines should be communicated immediately so that sales staff approaching a signature date are clear.

Digital trading is another valuable tool for you: a modern age is around the corner.

Long-term effects

What happens when we have CoVid-19 behind us, and things seem normal again?

First of all, actions to continue operating on a private basis could have had another objective: validating or refuting the sellers and consumers' claims about the need for informal connections. Where the procurement of travel that will profit more from face-to-facing interactions will return depending on company expectations and desires, where social isolation is no longer required. However, a small number of your customers may feel that it is no obstacle to the purchase/sale process. But why not continue to focus on what works?

Recommended action: identify customers and transactions most affected by 100% virtual use and proactively collect feedback on the shopping experience.

If the sales reps can continue selling in the long run, are they now sales reps?

Considering that social distance can also affect sales teams who typically work from the same office to distance themselves, the boundaries between sales representatives and sellers may not be blurred if both sellers sell houses. However, there is a difference between "virtual sales" and "internal sales." So the short answer is: No, a sales representative who sells without a face-to-face meeting will not be used as the term "internal seller."

Let's think about what distinguishes the back office from the field service

Although we typically use "Field Sales Reps" vs. "Inside Sales Reps" Due to organizational structures and compensation plans, it is an oversimplification to have a binary view. It is the complexity of the buyer's navigation on his journey that distinguishes internal sales from the sales force. For customers and transactions that can be standardized and repeatable, we simply took the next logical step, remotely distributing roles and specializing in the role to maximize repeatability and speed.

We were all caught up in the use of shorthand and the distinction between office staff and field staff based on the ability to sell remotely. However, as online collaboration becomes more common, a requirement that an employee encounters face-to-face can no longer act as a valid proxy for the complexity of sales experience required for the buyer's journey. Ask yourself the following question: Do the social distances due to CoVid-19 require more or fewer sales skills to group your higher value and more complex ways of closing while you are practically carrying out the whole process? Few, if any, would answer this question less. Therefore, it is worth noting that the reason we usually balance staff positions in the field more than internal positions is because of the skill required to close the deal, not a travel reward for personally meeting Meet customers.

Why is this distinction important?

Given the relentless cost constraints that impact selling companies, it is likely that certain people will exploit the chance if the social gap reveals that customers are purchasing in a phase to move consumers to an 'insider' model virtual. This could be the wrong step if a virtual interaction is misinterpreted without further changing the sales requirements as a signal to switch to a different sales movement or another type of sales resource for coverage. Therefore, a distinction can be made between what represents an "internal sales" model and what cannot be the difference between pen sharpening and creating a customer experience and a sales disaster.

Measures you should prepare when social distancing is no longer needed:

DO NOT rush to transfer customers to an internal team immediately or reclassify existing sales representatives as internal sales representatives

Experienced employees are likely to be allergic to termination within the sales rep. To identify cases where customers can switch to an internal sales model, it is necessary to examine the speed and complexity of the sales process, NOT just the willingness to shop virtually

Monitor the travel needs of your sales representatives to recalibrate your account coverage or meet capacity expectations.

As mentioned above, the perception (by the representative or the buyer) of what can be achieved practically without requiring the social distance experience of CoVid-19 can affect personal logistics. Virtual selling in itself does not simplify a purchase journey to allow the transition to an internal sales model. This saves time and money, and you want to determine how many additional customers a sales rep can cover

Expand the size of your area relatively based on the new forecast of your time availability (without driving/flying, an employee should be able to cover more customers).

SPEAK AN EXPERT: HOW TO SWITCH TO VIRTUAL SALES TO HELP YOUR COMPANY SURVIVE COVID-19

If you listen carefully, you may hear companies around the world wresting their predictions for 2020. With governments imposing bans for several months, we are likely to hear the effects on our lives, our businesses, and the economy for a while '. With the cancellation of all live events and conferences, companies that relied heavily on a personal network model were the first to support the burden.

Most firms will also re-evaluate ways of communicating and establishing genuine partnerships with customers. The first and clearest step is that more focus will be paid to physical space, and companies that embrace technologies more rapidly will benefit from the first engines.

Impact on sales: a changing landscape

B2B sales have traditionally been regarded as a personal and relationship-based part of the business relationship that the coronavirus has completely stopped in most cases. To survive in this new normal, vendors must replace traditional personal meetings and events with a virtual [sales] commitment.

This sales phase looks very different from a few months ago and requires a change in mentality, skills, and technology. To achieve profitability, businesses must develop techniques for engaging purchasers during the sales process and how to activate and assist employees in this new way of selling effectively.

To help companies succeed in this new normal, Your Story hosted the first Ask Me Anything (AMA) on April 29, 2020, with experts from LinkedIn, Freshworks, and HT Media on how to proceed with virtual sales.

Here are some key extracts from the session:

D. Virtual sales are the new normal, and everyone wants to understand the basics. What should companies focus on when they start this journey?

Neetu Singh: Traditional companies that access virtual sales due to the pandemic need to consider a few things. First, look at your sales funnel. The behavior of the buyer has changed because customers have also become virtual. We have to find out our strengths and find out what the ideal buyer's journey will look like from his point of view. Secondly, once we understand our customers' appearance, we need to create usable content suitable for each funnel stage. Third, there will be a change in consciousness. We accept the fact that webinars, blogs, etc. They are going well; in these difficult times, we have to change the mentality of the current team, and this will be a learning phase for everyone.

Question: Each transition to a new operating model involves some initial problems, and you have to adapt as a manager. What tactics and approaches would you recommend to others to follow in this new environment? How should they measure if they are doing well - for their company and teams?

Abhai Singh: Almost all companies in the world have had a Vision 2020 that has been discussed in its boardrooms. As in March, companies started to redefine their strategies. Every organization is looking at how they would do business in the market after COVID-19. I don't think there is a crystal ball that can predict what to do this time. However, there are some basic guiding principles.

For some, it may hold customers back. It could be for startups to raise awareness and seek new regions. The most critical thing is to speak with the clients to determine their impact and to define both short-term and long-term goals. If you understand it correctly, find out if your solution can help you overcome this crisis and talk to those who have sufficient data and knowledge. Be as creative as possible, and create unique models with the same or better chance of success than ever, and you never know which gold mine you could hit.

Question: What changes/changes in mentality should take into account more traditional industries such as printing [which depend even more on personal contacts] when moving to virtual sales? How should success feel here? And what should you do to measure company productivity and sales?

Ramesh Menon: I think it is an excellent time for traditional companies like ours to manage processes and ways of working. We have been selling physically for so long, and organizations like ours are very busy and need a lot of people. It is a perfect time to re-evaluate and eradicate any added value procedures and practices. Some processes slow down sales. Traditional companies like ours will think of investing more in technology. But we have to coordinate processes and technology. And that's the big change organizations like us have to make now.

Question: Today, there is a firm attitude in sales that we meet our customers for a coffee, and then we make this coffee a comfortable business. How easy is it to build an online relationship? Is there a change we need to get used to?

Abhai: Before discussing the mentality, I want to give you some facts. There has been a 153% rise in the number of customers living at home, not just in India, but also around the globe. Consequently, the conduct would change until the ban ends. It's clear one thing: three months ago it won't be here. It's not going to be there. The modern norm is that. Everything we do today will not be short-term but long-term. Companies need a long-term vision because things are sure to change. There will be situations where sales professionals have to talk to a customer and meet over coffee. But these things will be rare in the next six to twelve months. So if you need to keep your commitment, there must be more than just a change in mentality.

Question: How do you effectively manage this change and use systems and processes to manage change?

Ramesh: It's almost a daily conversation for us. How can traditional marketing teams understand why sales teams are entering marketing? This is the challenge we all face. The changes have to come from above, and I think change management has been introduced. People should stop asking wrong questions, especially those that are no longer relevant today. The bottom of the pyramid changes much faster if the guys above actually make that change.

Question: How can sales teams use digital technology/products to acquire or retain customers? Will this change drastically? How important are the right tools today?

Abhai: the buying behavior has changed dramatically. And there are many collaboration tools that people use that have suddenly become the new buzzwords. But if you take a step back, is it equally important to whom you speak? The populations of policymakers must be educated enough to consider. Around 46% of the population is projected to consist of civilizations in 2020. Seventy-three hundred of them agree on you. And their transactions should vary considerably from their previous generation. You will do a lot of research yourself before formulating an opinion. So I think the right digital tools will be the lifeblood for any sales organization to do three basic things. First of all, identify the right customer segment; Secondly, create more connections in the same organization than before COVID-19 and, thirdly, above all, how to stay in touch with them through data and insights during the sales cycle.

Neetu: tools are important because customers don't currently work in the office. Now, not only a data archive, everybody uses the CRM tool, just to understand what happens to the account. What did the company respond to campaigns? Therefore, sales servers, cheatsheets, models, etc. are available.

Question: In the race for fresh and trendy devices, what situations/accidents will businesses accept or avoid?

Ramesh: They have all the equipment, but with the right preparation, people have been offered the toughest obstacle. The only path, I assume, is contact. You should also focus on those who are not prepared to respond to transition. It 's important, and I guess because some people don't want this change. And letting them work in conventional industries is safer than battling. But you have to see how customers use it to educate teams in addition to investing in technology.

Success Plan While personal revenues could be behind us, maintaining partnerships over the years is more critical than ever. Sales managers have to develop and change their systems now to succeed. The best technologies and procedures would make it easy for vendors to turn to remote selling for those who first move into virtual selling, particularly because customers are often more effective.

DIGITAL ERA SALES: WHY EVERY SALES PROFESSIONAL MUST UNDERSTAND DIGITAL MARKETING

It is impossible to understand, but at times goods, services, and technologies have just been sold physically. Sellers were seen as the only door and touch person before, after, and after each transaction.

Quickly switch to today's digitally connected world, where people can learn almost anything about a product or service with just a few mouse clicks.

Today the world is driven by digital media, which is why almost all aspects of the sales process are surprisingly different. From prospecting, interviewing, and discussion to the introduction, agreement, and conclusion, everything has changed.

Digital-age sales mean that you understand the current new platforms and technology and that your web footprint can be easily used to attract, retain, and convert future customers.

You have to grasp digital marketing first to do so.

How Electronic Marketing requires Sales Professionals
HubSpot says:

"Online marketing includes all marketing efforts using a mobile system or the internet. businesses communicate with existing and future clients via digital platforms such as search engines, social media, e-mail, and websites."

A familiar sound? It needs to. You have the same aim as a sales specialist, but perhaps you have not thought about digital marketing that way.

You may think you don't need to know digital marketing because you are not looking for keywords, running campaigns, and optimizing results, but think again.

We addressed the importance of sales and marketing coordination during the past, which will keep coming to the fore, as the boundaries between these two divisions are no longer dissipating.

The most successful marketing and sales teams came together to form an operational revenue team. And for a good reason:

- Companies with tightly matched sales and marketing teams have 38% higher sales profit rates and 36% higher customer retention rates.
- When the sales and marketing departments collaborate, both parties aim to make money, and their attempts to accomplish the target are seamless.
- Companies with coordinated sales and marketing generate 208% more sales with marketing.
- Simply put better team alignment = more sales.

How does a trader consider digital marketing?

Because the internet has all changed, the production, distribution, and use of information has stopped in digital media. You have changed your position as a seller. It is more strategic and less transactional. More data and technical expertise are increasingly required.

Yet with the transition, there's a possibility. The opportunity to learn, develop, and improve.

From a sales perspective, you know if you are familiar with digital marketing:

- Better understand your ideal buyers

- Map your sales process and your approach to the buyer journey
- Understand intentions and interests better
- Ensure relevance and personalization
- Optimize the results

Let's review them one at a time to explain how each of them affects your sales process and your approach:

Better understand your ideal buyers

In marketing, this means that you know your buyer's personalities in reverse.

For a marketer, a buyer is an integral resource. You help your clients understand and make sure your communications (from sales e-mails and website materials to appropriate materials) are important.

A person is a semi-fictitious representation of your real and potential customers based on market research and data. A person reveals your customers' goals, motivations, behaviors, values, and weaknesses.

While this seems obvious, I'm always surprised by the number of sellers who don't have a good grip on the ideal buyer profile.

How does your business strategy boost your perception of this?

When you start looking at your contacts, potential customers, and customers from their perspective, you can connect and more effectively target their emotions as people, not just as buyers of your product, service, or solution.

You can even better qualify and prioritize leads because you know exactly who to talk to.

Map your sales process and your approach to the buyer journey

You can't give it all the same way.

One has different expectations in the early stages of the trip than the possibility of making a decision.

HubSpot defines the buyer journey as the process that buyers go through to know, evaluate, and buy a new product or service.

Traveling is a three-step process:
- Awareness phase: the buyer realizes he has a problem.

- Consideration phase: the buyer defines his problem and looks for ways to solve it.
- Decision phase: the buyer chooses a solution.

It could appear to be a very simple process, but it has become more complex in the new age. You will scan for your company, service, or solution and find the details about it.

For example, 60% of buyers prefer not to communicate with sales representatives as their primary source of information. And 68% of B2B customers prefer to do their research online.

Sales in the digital age have introduced new ways of connecting and collecting information. This is good in a way, but it also means that your buyers develop their opinions and prejudices. Where are you

How does the business strategy benefit from a deeper understanding?

You need your approach to diversified and modern learning as a sales specialist.

By planning the selling process and influencing the customer's experience, you will get the right details at an optimal moment, ask the best questions, and hit the correct social media platforms for potential consumers.

- Obtain the correct content at the right time: this would greatly boost the chance to deliver the best goods at the right moment by knowing the questions and insights that consumers seek.
- Just ask yourself the right questions: you are in the best place to find out more about how the customers are on the road to sales and how they can share details about the point of the trip and why. In addition to asking yourself better questions to understand the opportunity, when you have a deeper insight into the latest website or the potential customer's content, you are also asking better questions to the potential customer to guide the process seamlessly.
- Connect to the right social media platforms: social selling is a hot topic these days, and rightly so: social sellers offer 45% more opportunities than their colleagues, 51% more likely to reach odds and sell non-social one's Colleagues with 78% more than 78% all time. Social selling is

about connecting to your audience before buying your product or service. It is about providing resources that potential customers and customers know they can get not only product information but also industry trends and general education. In conclusion: sales representatives sell more on social media.

Understand intentions and interests better

Keyword research and knowledge of SEM and SEO practices are key to selling in the digital age.

In this case, a potential customer decides to look for generic terminology and not for the product, service, or business name if a potential customer searches (which Google says starts with roughly 71 percent).

The selling department will learn a lot about customers ' preferences and desires from this form of study and expertise when designing the website for this type of research.

Consumer behavior analysis indicates that trust is central to purchasing purposes. When trust is high, the chance and participation of people are even greater.

How does the business strategy benefit from a deeper understanding?

Your purchasers would like to deal with someone they can trust. You want a trustworthy and easy commodity, service, or solution.

From a sales perspective, you need to position yourself as a trusted consultant. When you sell in the digital age, you can do just that, but it requires perspective, digital thinking, and networking.

- Perspective: what is your perspective? In other words, what unique information or prospects do you offer to your potential customers and clients? Why should they trust you? Prepare your prospect by researching the industry, the company, and your contacts. What similar customers have you worked with, and could you share a case study or success story?
- Content: do you generate content that can be shared with potential customers and potential customers, whether it's a blog post or a video? You will gain popularity for reputation and authority when you build high-quality content,

which adds value to your audience. The clients don't like someone who is just a salesman but someone who's a professional.

- Networking: find out about the buyer's ideal personalities by remaining in their places, such as network activities or conferences. You can use it to improve your understanding of possible factors that cause the purchase.

Ensure pertinence and individualization

Professionals in digital marketing realize how critical it is to create meaningful and customized experiences.

Prices in the digital era are expected to grow regardless of B2C and B2B prices. When they approach you or another sales agent, your prospective clients make their decisions about you and your services. This makes customization even more difficult, but all the more necessary to stand out from the competition.

Consider these statistics:

- 65% of corporate customers say they would change brands if they didn't commit to personalizing their communications.
- 75% of corporate customers expect companies to anticipate their needs and make relevant suggestions by 2020.
- Custom e-mails have a purchase rate six times higher.
- 75 percent are more likely to shop from a seller that describes the store by name, offers products based on past sales, or has a history of sales.

How does the business strategy benefit from a deeper understanding?

Everyone likes a personalized experience. Your B2B buyers are no different. They are still consumers who are concerned with the way they buy everyday items. Amazon's convenience, Uber's lightness - all experiences influence their expectations - and now they expect the same simple shopping experience from you. You can customize the B2B experience through preparation, technology, and targeting.

- Preparation: do your homework. I can't stress it enough, but many sellers avoid this step. Take part in both planned and educated talks on potential developments in the industry so you can speak smartly about what is happening in your own country.
- Technology: top sellers use technology to evaluate whether the information they share with a buyer hits the mark. Using tools such as e-mail tracking and Point Drive, sales representatives can see where a buyer is located and what a buyer is ignoring by providing a feedback loop. You can then use this information to personalize future interactions.
- Targeting: Sales professionals can use social media platforms to segment potential buyers through features like advanced filters, demographic information, and lead bots to facilitate the identification of qualified leads further.

Optimize your results

Measurement is the first move to the results: how large and effective was the campaign? How many consumers did various marketing platforms see, press, and convert? You will examine the marketing data to see how the strategy works in a broad and in-depth manner. In this way, you can understand both the minor components and the main components of the campaign and determine whether they were successful.

Data-driven companies report significant improvements in decision making three times more often. 62% of executives rely even more on experience and advice than data when making decisions.

What is measured is managed. For this reason, companies that focus on data and measurements know how to optimize and improve. I can analyze the data and identify feasible insights.

How does the business strategy benefit from a deeper understanding?

Marketing and revenue data is a valuable treasure chest. The more you can evaluate, perceive, and determine, the more time and expectations you can handle.

You have revenue goals or thresholds as a marketing agent, but are you still following them? You have to chart your revenue and set your objectives.

For example, it is possible to set numeric targets for qualified leads, phone calls, meetings, suggestions, etc. Some of these may be weekly goals. Others may be monthly or quarterly.

And now? Digital and customer-oriented thinking

You cannot sell to someone at a different stage of the purchase path in the same way. You have to understand where I am and therefore adapt your strategy accordingly.

Customer-oriented thinking means support, offers, and products that match the buyer's exact location on the road to purchase.

To meet expectations, a complete customer vision is needed, promoted by a good understanding of the data and the alignment of sales and marketing. In this way, orientation is beneficial for both the customer and the company. 54% of sales and marketing professionals say they work together as a financial performance booster.

REACH CUSTOMER ATTENTION THROUGH DIGITAL TRANSFORMATION

Important points

- The switch to digital involves a paradigm shift from a traditional product-oriented strategy to one that focuses more on the customer
- Numerous customer data are isolated and hidden in various silos throughout the company
- If you use it and integrate it for further information and contextual measures, the customer experience can be highlighted to make every contact point relevant

In the next five years, most of the companies that are now in the latest technology era will be becoming the first digital business. A fascinating question to ask us for a break is: what is digitalization? A plurality (87%) of businesses worldwide see digital transition rather than customer-oriented competition as a business advantage. This can be perceived because technology and results play an exceptional role in most digital transformations.

Customer service was, therefore, an important element in the phase of transition. We live today in a hyper-connected world where knowledge is commodities, the internet is the supply chain, and the cloud is the storehouse. The transformation into digital means that the conventional product-oriented strategic approach must eventually change toward one, which focuses more on the consumer. The digitalization would bring a new age of sophisticated methods to create technologies that require and provide customers with added value.

Product centricity vs. attention to the customer

So far, many companies have defined themselves through the products they produce or the services they offer, rather than the problems they solve. A product-oriented company essentially deals with the superiority of the product, an approach more guided by research and technology.

On the other hand, a customer-oriented company focuses on diagnosing business problems and offers value through customized solutions. It is an external approach based on experiences of providing innovative services to meet the emotional needs of the customer. The main focus here is on a long-term relationship, and it's more about the customer's thinking share than the market share. In terms of strategy, customer orientation, therefore, follows a buyer-oriented pull approach rather than a sales-oriented push approach. Mass media tools such as TV, OOH billboards, and print (to increase product awareness) are giving way to new digital media tools such as influencers, marketing experience, and personalized travel to encourage user engagement. Apple is a good example of a product-oriented company. In Steve Jobs's words: "Customers don't know what they want until you show them." This idea forms the core of Apple's organizational and market structure, which allows the most effective and profitable delivery of its highly innovative products to its customers. Individual customer feedback is less emphasized, and the same product features are available to anyone who can pay.

Amazon is on the other end of this spectrum. Jeff Bezos summarizes the e-commerce giant's philosophy: "If you focus on competitors, you have to wait for a competitor to do something. If you are customer-focused, you can do pioneering work." All Amazon does is turn around, taking care of customer joy. You can argue that they have no products to sell, but have worked for customer attention through their unique service delivery platform.

Place your client in the center

A market full of many goods and services is a struggle to achieve a competitive edge. Therefore, it is important in the market for the benefit to establish specific characteristics and compensate for volume and value. The comparative advantage of those who best understand the desires and concerns of their clients.

This requires listening to customers, their response, and their involvement, especially in the early stages. Monetizing efforts in the customer experience journey too early can lead to an early end. Also, companies cannot include all customers in a collection segment and pursue the same communication, engagement, sales, and CRM strategy for everyone.

As the Pareto principle implies, 80 percent of a company's sales are likely to come from 20 percent of its customers. It will not be fair to treat segments of this quality in the same way as casuals, hikers, or impulse buyers. Digital transformation allows all factors on a customer's purchase path - awareness, leads, recommendations, and final purchase - to be assigned to a channel or segment of customers.

To this end, the value of the customer's life is an effective and critical measure of corporate sustainability. If you pay attention to customer acquisition and retention costs and focus on upselling and cross-selling, you can increase customer revenue and loyalty at optimized costs.

Illustration of the customer journey

The journey of the digital customer begins with answers to simple questions.

- What makes my customers special?
- What are your contact points in the customer journey? How do you use them?
- What do they appreciate and expect?
- Who or what influences them? Who do they influence?

Technology does not define digital transformation, but it is a sure means for better customer experience. As consumers and technology come together, customer value emerges. This occurs when an organization only follows the direction of the customer from the viewpoint of the consumer.

This made Starbucks so good. Look at the customer's journey from the customer's point of view. This led them to discover nine different areas of the workflow connected due to the customer journey. Starbucks changed the intersectoral workflow and collaboration processes accordingly.

Find out how digital allows customer orientation

The core of digital transformation is really about customers and their experiences. And the key to digital transformation is there for everyone. Large customer data is isolated and hidden in various silos throughout the company. If you use it and integrate it for further information and contextual measures, the customer experience can be highlighted to make each contact point relevant. Let's take a look at the many options.

Content optimization and channel activation

In the modern world of marketing, content is king. For a millennium or Gen Z consumers, content optimization is all the more important. The "digital native" has very little time to process advertisements and is usually connected to one or more digital devices. Highly qualified leads can be generated by displaying ads in a format typical of the user's device or with the content of particular interest to this segment. Understanding user online behavior is key.

Facebook takes care of the content in the news feed taking into account past activities to maintain relevance. The click flow analysis on news websites allows the dynamic rendering of articles of interest to the user. Brands use data about users' online behavior through re-marketing platforms to place targeted ads for a higher click-through rate. Platforms with a large amount of user data, such as Twitter, can exchange information with a variety of tools and software via structured request-response data lines, the so-called APIs. Digital and social media platforms certainly can track and fully share user behavior to obtain a better strategy for activating content and channels.

Another positive example of content management is Kraft's symbiotic relationship with Pinterest. Kraft arrived in 2012 at Pinterest when he learned that the service had a large audience. Because recipes are one of Pinterest's most common interests, Kraft's mission has been to make regular and inexpensive meals easier for people to find. Pinterest today is a powerful Kraft tool that enables you to obtain real-time insights and extracts information and influence content development and care for your customers.

Insights and analysis

The wide variety of data companies can access a direct benefit of digital transformation. Analyzing visit data on the website through conceptual research offers useful information about improving website quality and navigation. Likewise, most ECs improve their queue, checkout, and transaction efficiency visibility, with data modified in real-time. This simplifies tactical options and reduces market time.

The North Face, American outdoor clothing, equipment, and footwear company, uses artificial intelligence technology to help online shoppers find the right jacket selection from the thousands of item numbers on their website. This online experience allows customers to have a question and answer conversation to find the right jacket. You have created an experience that comes close to interacting with a human sales representative.

Crowdfunding initiatives include customer opinions at each stage and facilitate product development. Local auto company Local Motors is reinventing the way cars are designed and built. They get valuable information from their online customer community.

Digitization allows a uniform 360-degree view from multiple data sources (online, retail, sales, surveys to track consumer brands and attitude studies) to identify precisely defined customer segments and adapt strategies targeting.

Social listening

Social media provide data on the level of awareness and involvement of your content and offer the opportunity to listen to the consumer's voice in an unrestricted environment. Of course, there are several challenges, such as irrelevant content, spam, and ambiguous hues. Advanced tools that process social media data using complex text mining algorithms can contextualize conversations and assign them to conversations (positive, negative, or neutral). This paves the way for scalable early warning systems, influencer disclosure, and customer response management.

With the social media analytics platform SocioSEER developed by WNS, its customers' brand can increase its objectives in terms of brand value, customer orientation, and sales. The NoSQL back-end architecture and summary engines allow for scalability and speed. SocioSEER uses advanced analysis and machine learning frameworks to obtain content classification and indexing. It offers a graphic-rich display in the frontend and simplifies brand marketing to classify relevant social conversations and impressions accurately. It helps collect data, information, and social conversations around a brand and provides a deeper subdivision of what they mean.

Bring human stories to the foreground

With the increase in global Internet penetration and mobile devices, digital transformation has undoubtedly paved the way for a business strategy that aims to improve the customer experience. It is certainly a paradigm shift that has allowed people to have a say and influence strategic decisions.

The truth is that digital transformation is not just a shift in technology investments. All over the world, we see companies using digital roadmaps with the technology and resources available in their respective country-specific conditions. Ultimately, relevance is the fundamental criterion for transformation, and it is based on this

- Appreciation of digital consumer development
- Clarity in the visualization of changing markets

- Leadership to take advantage of emerging consumer and market opportunities and make customer-centric changes

Customer orientation is the new normality of competitive advantage. No cost No product differentiation. Customer proximity helps companies overcome competition noise and disorder. Since digital and social issues have irreparably upset the corporate landscape, the customer is the only way to succeed. It remains to be seen whether product-oriented companies will continue to assert themselves against a stronger customer voice or move towards a digital-oriented customer-oriented approach.

VIRTUAL SALES SERVICES

HOW TO GET ONLINE PURCHASES IN 6 SIMPLE MEASURES

You aren't alone if you dream of making a difference as an online seller, but you don't know how to market online.

Some brilliant ideas and potential contractors were misled about online purchases.

How to begin sales online in six steps

1. Select a killer commodity or build one

2. Compile a Publicity Campaign online

3. How to find the best eCommerce site for online selling?

4. Build your e-commerce website

5. Live your marketing strategy

6. Measure your results

For those who have just started, figuring out how to start an online business in the e-commerce world can be a confusing mess.

Thanks to our detailed and accurate checklist for the launch and management of a profitable online shop, we will help you stop noise and become an online seller.

This is the tutorial for you if you've always wanted to learn how to market your e-commerce shop online, but don't learn how to get going.

1. Select a killer commodity or build one

Some people earn millions of dollars from senseless goods due to their single marketing strategy (I think of Pet Rock). However, if you have a great product or, even better, several great products, it will be much easier to succeed if you learn how to start selling online. Choose the perfect place for a relaxed feeling. Test that the company is not competitive (but marketable) and has reasonable margins for sales.

Many independent businesses have one way or another to offer services. You can mix expertise on the sale of online resources, ranging from advanced instruction to professional assistance to personal coaching.

When you create an online business, keep in mind that products like video tutorials, individual advice, or step-by-step plans can be incredibly interesting for customers.

Are you currently running a small business? While brainstorming product ideas, think about where your company already stands out and what you may want to expand.

If you sell original greeting cards locally, you should print shirts or socks with a similar style and messages. Are you now an online math seller? To order to boost tutoring, try adding an eBook.

The wheel must not be reinvented to switch from internet selling to very productive company construction. Most online retailers sell incredibly effective scripting items, and this is the starting point of most entrepreneurs.

The best way to learn how to begin online selling is by purchasing bulk goods from wholesalers. You can find a range of extremely cheap items using websites such as Alibaba.com.

Another great option for an online seller who keeps operating and shipping costs low are digital products.

Digital products include e-books, games, online courses, etc.

With digital products, you don't have to worry about shipping, inventory management, or anything else during the sale of physical products.

The best thing about it is that digital downloads are already a quick seller, and others will opt for items like 0,0 on a device. Know what your unique talent is, and you are on the road to online shopping.

2. Put together a marketing plan for online sellers

Wondering how to sell online? It's about marketing. Gone are when an online seller could simply open a website, sit back, and watch the traffic. While it is possible to build an online store that sees a lot of traffic - and sales - you will have to skip the line to get there. Fortunately, learning how to start an online business has many marketing strategies that you can use to direct people to your website, including:

- PPC advertising
- Social media marketing
- Blog and content marketing

- Create backlinks
- E-mail marketing
- Search engine optimization (SEO)
- Affiliate marketing
- Video marketing

You want to learn as much about Online Marketing Tactics as possible and develop a personalized digital marketing strategy.

It is important to create an online marketing plan before actually creating your website and selling online, as the marketing plan you create can affect your website's design. Select one of these marketing ideas from the list above that it seems interesting to you. Instead, continue studying and playing with ads.

3. How to find the best eCommerce site for online selling?

You will boost and impact your online shop on the right e-commerce site. We addressed what you want to find on our E-Commerce website in one of our previous posts. These include, in summary:

- Excellent customer service

- Strong aesthetics
- Useful functions
- A good user interface
- Maximum security
- Affordable prices

Take the time to discover the sites and pick not one alone. Not all platforms are identical, and you are building the whole business in an e-commerce network system. Make sure that you pick one that gives you what you need for a good online store.

4. Build your e-commerce website

After learning something about selling online and choosing a great e-commerce platform, it's time to create your website. While choosing a platform with a variety of tools and an intuitive interface greatly simplifies creating a good website, you still need to invest a lot of time and effort in optimizing the website. We could write whole books (and many have) on optimal web design, but there are some bases from which every online seller should start. First of all, you want to add sharp, enticing photographs and excellent written material to your e-commerce platform.

Customers deserve to learn that they are buying from a professional, and there's nothing that shouts like terrible photos and poorly-described items. Take the time to find lovely images, write wonderful ingredients, and add this stuff to your web so you can see them quickly.

So you want to sell your products. If you've chosen a good e-commerce platform, this step is simple, and features like checkout and payment options are already available. What you have to do is list the goods, upload product photos and specifications, and select pricing and delivery choices.

Recall that minor choices will have a big effect on your online shop if you are comfortable with the online learning curve. Think SEO, sign forms, testimonials, and all other things you may market, and you are done. There's something else to consider when you want to start selling online. Sales at Omnichannel are an innovative way to suggest that both online and offline connect with your clients. Consequently, building a global experience is critical.

Your company will generate more sales if your customers can access your products and information about your products from different entry points.

For example, with an e-commerce platform that offers embeds, you can include articles for sale directly on your blog. With a button or widget, your customers get the same simple payment process that you created on your e-commerce website. A Facebook store is also an excellent idea for any online seller. Start with the online area you are most involved in and expand from there.

5. Go live with your marketing plan

Now that the online shop is in development, it's time for consumers on the new e-commerce website to show their marketing plan. The preference of marketing strategies depends to a large degree, whether and how you sell online.

Whatever you pick, one thing is important: your marketing plan must be versatile as an online seller. Changes are unavoidable if you want to learn how to launch and run an online company. Many tactics work well, and other campaign techniques do not work. Be vigilant to analyze and adjust the promotional campaign.

Don't sweat if the marketing strategy you use is completely different from the one you initially implemented. This trial and error development of your online marketing approach is part of building a successful online store.

6. Measure your results

The most successful online seller always learns how to start selling online and is always looking for ways to improve.

The internet is continually changing, and, if it dies, more information will still exist than anyone internet retailer will possibly have.

When you get more information about starting up an online business, the more important your actions become to calculate the progress. You know how to sell online after reading this article, and it is now time to explore what works best.

Try new tactics, review your data, and make changes. Never be complacent.

THE MINIMUM REQUIREMENTS TO CREATE A COMMERCIAL ACTIVITY

When starting a new business, entrepreneurs should make sure that they meet all the legal responsibilities of running a small business. New businesses and startups are subject to a range of regulatory standards, including banking controls, tax laws, and labor legislation. Ensure your new client's ethical requirements are fulfilled, and you are free to concentrate on building your business again.

Which are the legal requirements for beginning a company?

You may have a brilliant new business plan, but first, you have to make sure that the legal conditions are met to open a company to launch a company. Here is a guidance document for legalizing your company, which is easy to understand:

CREATE AN LLC OR CORPORATION

The first legal requirement that you must meet as a new entrepreneur is the choice of your company's business structure. You can choose between the foundation of an LLC or a company. Both structures have advantages and disadvantages. So do your research before choosing a business structure for your startup.

- LLC: In most cases, an LLC or a limited liability company protects you from criminal responsibility. It means your financial belongings, including house and cars, are not in jeopardy if your business is sued or declared bankrupt. You would have to pay an LLC, so you will also get a self-employment allowance to disclose your corporation earnings as part of your federal income tax.

- Company: a company or company, C is a company legally an entity separate from its owner or owners. Companies offer the highest level of protection of personal responsibility from all corporate structures. However, they are more expensive and more complicated to model. Companies apply a separate income tax to their profits.

The Small Business Administration has created a useful guide for different business structures and the advantages and disadvantages of individual options.

Register your trade name

The name of the corporation must be registered before a legal arrangement is agreed upon. Select a name that represents the brand and ensure that it is not yet demanded. Your business will then be licensed. This is registered in four forms, each for its purposes:

- Company name: protect your company legally at the state level
- A brand: legally protects your company at the federal level
- A DBA (do business like): it does not offer legal protection, but it can vary depending on the position and the corporate structure
- A domain name: specify your company's web address

Request a federal tax code

The federal tax identification number is called the Employer Identification Number (EIN). You can lawfully hire employees, pay income taxes, apply for business licenses, and open a business bank account. **The IRS website will apply for an EIN. Your company needs an EIN if you want to:**

- Hire and pay employees
- Presentation of the employer's tax return
- Act like a company
- Using a deferred tax plan

Determine if a tax ID number is needed

Check if your startup needs a tax code. You only need it if the state in which you operate collects corporation tax. As tax obligations vary from state to state, it is best to visit your state's website and check local income tax and labor tax laws.

GET PERMITS AND COMMERCIAL LICENSES

Federal and state business licenses and permits must be applied for. However, the specific licenses required to depend on your business's industry and the location of your business. Small Business Administration has a list of general industry licenses required by the industry. This is a strong basis for your studies. The licenses and permits available at the national level and the fees owed, depending on the position and the key business activities. State and state study requires, depending on the position of the business.

PROTECT YOUR COMPANY WITH INSURANCE

Corporate insurance can protect you in cases where your specific corporate structure's protection of personal liability is insufficient. Corporate insurance can protect not only your assets but also your corporate assets. Other forms of insurance, such as joblessness and disability insurance, are mandated by statute. It's always a smart thing to safeguard the enterprise from any future threats. Some common options for business insurance are:

- General Liability Insurance: protect your business from various forms of financial loss,

including property damage, injury, health problems, dispute resolution or judgments
- Product Liability Insurance: This policy protects you if a product fails and injures consumers if the business sells products.
- Commercial property insurance: Covers your business from injuries or harm incurred by natural disasters, accidents, or destruction on your land.

OPEN A BUSINESS BANK ACCOUNT

From a legal point of view, before you receive payments from consumers, it is necessary to distinguish your personal and company finances. Choose a convenient bank and meet your needs, possibly by offering lower corporate rates to small business customers. After selecting a banking institution, you will need to open some information about your company to open an account, including:
- Identification number of your employer (or social security number for a single owner of your employer)

- The basic documents for your business
- Your commercial license
- Documents relating to the property contract

CONSULT THE PROFESSIONALS

To ensure that you have met all your new commercial legal obligations, you should seek professional advice. Sit separately with an attorney and an accountant to ensure your company is legally and financially secure before starting the business.

Can I start a company without registering it?

You must first register your company name to use this name for your company. If you don't have a company name registered with the Foreign Minister, you can only do business with your name. Before submitting your company name, make sure another person is not currently using it. Then register the name online through the IRS.

DIGITAL TRANSFORMATION: FREE DIGITAL TRANSFORMATION GUIDE

Improved and strategic incorporation of emerging technology, systems, and capabilities at each level and functions reflects economic, systemic, and operational transition within an enterprise, industry, or ecosystem.

Digital transformation (also DX or DT) uses technologies to create value and new services for various stakeholders (customers in a broad sense), to develop innovations and acquire the ability to adapt quickly to changing circumstances.

While digital transformation is mainly used in the business context, it also affects other organizations, such as governments, government agencies, and organizations that are involved in addressing social challenges such as pollution and population aging using one or more of these existing technologies and emerging.

Digital transformation isn't just about interference or technology. It's about value, people, optimization, and the ability to adapt quickly through the intelligent use of technology and information when needed.

In some countries like Japan, digital transformation also aims at affecting all facets of life with the country's Society 5.0 initiative (which bears some parallels to Industry 4.0's dream of industrial transformation).

The digital transformation reflects the fundamental transformation of business and organizational processes, strategies, capabilities, and systems to take full advantage of strategic and priority ways of taking into account current and future innovations, the evolutions, and opportunities of a mix of emerging technologies and their growing impact on society.

The development of new skills revolves around the ability to be more agile, person-oriented, innovative, customer-oriented, leaner, more efficient and able to induce/change opportunities to change the status quo and always to use big data and new data More unstructured use of source-oriented and service-oriented revenue, with the Internet of Things a crucial factor. Digital transformation activities and plans are also more urgent and are found in highly marketable markets.

Various causes can cause the current and future changes and changes that lead to the need for faster implementation of a digital transformation strategy, often simultaneously, in terms of customer behavior and expectations, new economic realities, social changes (aging Groups population), disturbance of the ecosystem/industry and (growing acceptance and innovation in terms of) emerging or existing digital technologies.

In practice, end-to-end optimization of customer experience, operational flexibility, and innovation are important drivers and objectives of digital transformation, as well as the development of new sources of income and ecosystems based on the value of information, which lead to transformations of the business model and new forms of digital processes. However, before you get there, you also need to resolve internal challenges, including those related to legacy systems and process disruptions, with inevitable internal goals for the next steps.

Digital transformation is a journey with several interconnected intermediate objectives, which ultimately aims at the ubiquitous optimization between processes, departments and the corporate ecosystem of a hyper-connected era in which the right bridges are built (between front-end and back-office, Data from things) and decisions, people, teams, technologies, various actors in ecosystems, etc.) are the key to success in the function of this journey.

The human dimension plays a major part in all stages in the transition processes (collaboration, environments, skills, community, empowerment, and so on) and, naturally, in the digital transformation objectives. Since people don't want "digital" for everything and practice human value and personal interactions, there will always be an "offline" element depending on the context. But even with non-digital interactions and transactions, digital transformation plays a role in empowering every customer-oriented agent and employee.

A strategy for digital transformation aims to create opportunities, to exploit the opportunities and opportunities of new technologies and their effects in a faster, better, and more innovative way in the future. A journey towards digital transformation requires a multi-layered approach with a clear roadmap involving a variety of stakeholders beyond the silos and internal/external constraints. This roadmap considers that the ultimate goals will continue to move because digital transformation is an ongoing journey, as is digital change and innovation.

In this online guide, we examine the essence of digital transformation as a vision for this journey, its developments, and its presence in various processes and business sectors.

Digital business transformation: a holistic approach

A holistic view of the myriad "digital" changes and programs at different levels in the enlarged organization's various divisions is the secret to the new transformation's success.

Digital technologies - and how we use them in our personal lives, in our work, and in society - have changed the face of business and will continue to do so. It was always the case, but the speed of change in the companies is accelerating and faster.

Perhaps the best word to characterize the complexities it encompasses is not digital transformation. Others prefer the term transformation of digital business that closely corresponds with the corporate dimension. As a general term, however, digital transformation is also used for changes of meaning that do not affect companies in the strict sense, but developments and changes in government and society, regulations, and economic conditions, and associated challenges, the so-called new disruptive disruptors. It is clear that changes/changes in society have an impact on organizations and, as such, can be very destructive if transformations are viewed from a holistic perspective. No company, no industry, no economic actor/stakeholder, and no area of society is isolated.

It is important always to recognize the generic dimension of the term digital transformation. Maturity models for digital transformation may be useful for defining visions, but they are too simple and general in practice.

Digital transformation involves a variety of processes, interactions, transactions, technological developments, changes, internal and external factors, industries, stakeholders, etc. I know that reading digital transformation recommendations or reading reports and forecasts is important to take them into account. Although there are common challenges, goals, and characteristics in organizations worldwide, there are huge differences for industry, the region, and the organization. What might make sense in one region should not make sense in another, even if we only look at the regulatory environment.

This guide is primarily concerned with transforming the digital business. That is, by turning into a digital market environment where the focus is moved to the margins of the company ecosystem. In this equation of customer engagement, employee satisfaction, stakeholder value/results, alliances, and a distinctly customer-oriented approach, the company has become a central factor in the broadest sense (external and internal with limits between the two uncertainties).

Developments and technological technologies ranging from cloud computing to big data, to advanced analysis, to artificial intelligence, to machine learning and to mobility/mobility (an important pioneer) towards the Internet of Things and new realities there are 1) that allow digital transformation and 2) causes of the needs of digital transformation (among other things, because they influence consumer behavior or transform entire sectors, such as in the digital transformation of production and 3) accelerators for innovation and transformation. Yet technology is just part of the solution since, by definition, digital transformation is holistic.

Digital transformation and hyperconnectivity: attention to the edges

Customer and customer experience, purpose and end objectives, partners, stakeholders, the last mile of processes, and interruptions often sit and occur on these edges and are the key to digital transformation. Sometimes the digital transformation is even limited to the customer experience, but strictly speaking, this is a mistake in which some other aspects are excluded.

The business, customers, and stakeholders, however, define the plan in its ultimate objectives. As interaction is the rule, the key role of the organization is to connect the points and transcend the inner silos in all areas to achieve these various goals. Although the focus shifts to the edges, the central functions are implemented to work faster and better for and on the edges. For example, this happens at an organizational (integrated, ecosystem), technological (as-a-service) level, enabling the cloud and agility and at a cultural level.

In IT technologies and paradigms such as edge computing and decentralization of work and business models, the transition towards the borders is also reflected.

Imagine how much data processing and analytics in a field where real-time demands are increasing as cloud computing increases, knowledge management becomes decentralized, protection becomes moved to endpoints, and more.

However, this does not mean that strategic decisions are marginalized or that digital transformation is only possible in organizations with "new" organizational models. Digital transformation at the company level includes leadership, irrespective of the enterprise, and the de facto differences that prevail between truth and perception and the systematic approach to achieving the goals, taking into account weaknesses and interiors. In realistic terms, we see this mostly from the bottom-up, ad hoc, or in some units, pilot projects on the road to a more central, company-wide approach. This is normal, typical for the early stages, but if it is not done on a larger scale, it is a potential risk of long-term success. From the same holistic imperative, one must also bear in mind that security requires a holistic vision and even a strategy for cyber resilience. Data is stored everywhere, attacks increase, and technological environments become more complex.

Digital transformation areas

The integrated and linked sense of digital transformation needed can include:

- Business activities: marketing, sales, staff, management, client support, etc.
- Business processes: one or more similar procedures, activities, and sets to achieve a particular business target where business process

management, business process optimization, and business process automation (innovations such as robotic automation) play a significant role. The optimization of business processes is fundamental for digital transformation strategies. Most industries and cases today are a mix of internal and customer-oriented goals.

- Business models: how companies work, from the market launch approach to the value proposition up to how they make money and want to effectively transform their core business by opening new sources of income and approaches and sometimes even leaving the traditional behind core business for a while.

- Corporate ecosystems: networks of partners and stakeholders, as well as contextual factors, affect the business, such as regulatory and economic priorities and developments. New ecosystems are created between companies with different backgrounds based on transformation and digital information, with usable data and information that become resources for innovation.

- Management of corporate resources: the focus is on traditional resources, but increasingly on less "material" resources such as information and customers (improving the customer experience is a primary objective of many digital transformation "projects" and l Information is the lifeblood of businesses .) Technological developments and any human relationships). Both customers and information must be treated as real goods from every perspective.
- Organizational culture, according to which there must be a clear, customer-oriented, agile, and hyper-conscious goal, which is obtained by acquiring key skills in areas such as digital maturity, leadership, knowledge worker silos, etc., which allow getting more future proof. Culture also overlaps with processes, commercial activities, collaboration, and the IT side of digital transformation. Changes are needed to bring the applications to market faster. This is the essence of DevOps: development and functioning. Changes are required (not only

knowledge and organizational methods but also procedures, culture, and collaboration), etc., for IT and OT to collaborate in businesses, procedures, or activities.

- Ecosystem and partnership models, including an increase in cooperative, collaborative, co-creation, and, last but not least, completely new approaches to corporate ecosystems that lead to new business models and sources of income. Ecosystems will be critical to the as-a-service economy and the success of the digital transformation.

- Customer, worker, and partner approach. Digital transformation puts people and strategies ahead of technology. The changing behavior, expectations, and needs of all stakeholders are crucial. This is expressed in many change sub-projects, where customer orientation, user experience, employee development, new business models, changing sales partner dynamics, etc. are expressed. (can) everyone enters the photo. It is important to note that digital technologies are never the only answer to addressing one of these human aspects, from employee satisfaction to improving the customer experience. People primarily involve, respect, and empower other people. Technology is an additional pioneer and part of the equation of choice and basic needs.

The list is not exhaustive, and the different things alluded to are directly related and overlapping. Let's examine some phenomena less related to "digital transformation" and the so-called interruptions related to the business world. Still, the attention is turned to business, which by definition, means a holistic vision of digital transformation, in which instead aspects such as customer experience, technological developments, and innovation with a clear purpose of a slogan are crucial elements.

There are no misfunctions or technologies all alone in digital transformation. It's not just about changing for a digital age. If it were the latter, you have to recognize that this digital age has existed for some time and is relatively vague.

Digital disruption: what is it anyway?

Digital disruption has been used not as one of the most frequent terms (as digital transformation did), but mainly because it is used in a business, an organization, or an environment, for instance, a corporation. Existing (mainly technical), newcomers or established companies who have mastered the skills of the digital business and have developed solutions, business models and approaches that lead to a significant change in customer behavior and the market context and they require existing actors (including "digital societies") that face significant challenges"). their strategies also change.

However, the outages are certainly not just about newcomers' initiatives or established companies with disruptive approaches. In the end, the interruptions concern people, customers.

Or, as Charlene Li says: the breakup is ultimately a shift in power in relationships. Ailments as a human phenomenon are caused, among other things, by changes in the way people use technology and by changes in their behavior and expectations. These changes can be brought about by new technologies and how they are adopted or used by disruptive new arrivals. The change can, however, also have a wider background with no technology. Does "internet interference" still exist? No. Nevertheless, emerging technologies may, in some cases, be used to resolve such behavior changes or expectations/needs, etc.

As Sameer Patel points out, there are often outages in the last mile of the customer experience. We would like to say that technical problems in general often occur at different limits of the business. The same margins we just mentioned: the last mile, the customer, the largest ecosystem, etc. Within the wider ecosystem, it is important to examine the disruptive effects that can influence, for example, the change in economic realities and regulations and underline the need to advise on digital transformation in the right light.

As we have discussed earlier, the reality that digital transformation always focuses on edges seems evident when looking at defects and cutting-edge expectations (customer expectations, technology staff at the end of business processes, etc.) that drive digital transformation.

Techs are often assumed to be unchanging. Yet it's a little inspirational to humans, to be frank.

We prefer to say that it is how technology is adopted and used that, as mentioned, can be disruptive. However, if we drop this small observation that these technologies are not disruptive, it is obvious that some technologies have caused more interference than others. We have mentioned a few. Social has been a great turning point. Furniture, which certainly leads to being mobile, is also one of these. Cloud. Big data analysis. Indeed, all the so-called third platform technologies and their accelerators have a key role in information and artificial intelligence.

In recent years, the evolution towards the Internet of Services and, yes, the Internet of Transformation, which will be the Internet of Things or the Internet of Things, has played a fundamental role in digital transformation. The Internet of Things and IoT, however, is still in its infancy, in which we move to the next level on the internet. Another unimportant word for connecting devices with integrated and wired networking, and the possibilities for the collection, transmission, processing, and reception of data through internet technology, is the nature of the internet. It is the catalyst for the rest of the manufacturing processes at the same time. The internet of things in consumer applications until now gave no real benefit or true innovation. The main value is found in the industrial Internet of Things, with industrial markets such as manufacturing and logistics that become leaders in the transformation. The latter is also due to technologies that are gradually demonstrating their disruptive potential, including additive manufacturing and advanced robotics.

Is there a stage afterward? Sure. At the moment, we will be completely hybrid in every way, including integrating digital technologies in our human self, which will be the fourth platform. Scary for many and certainly not for the next few years. But we will do it.

If you ask us what the next disruptive technologies will be (taking into account the details we have mentioned): it is the Internet of Things, together with cognitive/artificial intelligence systems, big data, and intelligence. In the meantime, the hybrid phase is already here, for example, in an industrial context in which the cyber-physical system. Therefore, the IoT (industrial) is a key component of Industry 4.0 and the industrial internet. However, human value and the human element remain the key at all times.

With digital transformation, the existing business is managed and built for the future at the same time; for example, the aircraft engine during the flight (Ashutosh Bisht, IDC).

Causes of interruptions and transformations

"Several factors can cause disruptions" and digital (corporate) transformation:

- Technological (technology-induced) innovations that are more effective than ever. However, it is not technology that drives a disorder or transformation. Customers, associates, rivals, and different stakeholders use and implement it. Technologies with clear interference potential include IoT, artificial intelligence, edge computing, virtual and augmented reality, and blockchain. However, the most disruptive potential is when they are combined and enable new applications, as we can see from the convergence of AI, IoT, and big data analysis. The combination of IT and OT is also changing the game in industrial transformation.

- Customer behavior and requirements. This so-called customer transformation and disruption is not necessarily related to technology. Technology frequently makes or develops technology when implemented and turned into business challenges, as described above. An example of digital transforming power is not powered by technology but only integrated into conjunction with other factors: consumer demand is far older than today in easy handling and simplicity. It is from the days when the internet did not exist. In this sense, digital transformation can also easily recover ground since companies no longer have other options (it is not as if they did not know how important it was to make customer interaction and support simple and fluid decades ago). Social disruptions can also influence customer behavior and needs.

- Innovative and creative. Completely new approaches to human and business challenges and innovations and inventions that create a new reality, be it in science, business, technology, or even in a non-technological context of true innovation, can be disruptive. The invention of drugs that change health care and society (as has happened several times in the past), the press, and the train can come next? The best choice is probably in the life sciences and the application of technology to the human body and mind.
- Induced by the ecosystem. Corporate environments and habitats, in which they-and we-work, are part of a larger environment, organizations. Economic changes, requirements of partners who want to adapt, developments towards collaboration in transformative corporate ecosystems, regulatory changes (e.g., the transformative effects of the General Data Protection Regulation or the GDPR),

geopolitical changes, social changes, unforeseen events such as natural disasters or even a pandemic, as COVID's impact on digital transformation and society as a whole has shown, can all influence and guide the need for digital transformation, as demonstrated by in-depth research to accelerate the digital transformation into the new normal.

And this aspect of the ecosystem brings us back to this essential aspect of digital transformation: the interdependence and networking of everything - and based on the need to think holistically, across sectors, and taking into account current and future changes, as already mentioned.

Everything overlaps and is connected, from interruptions, processes, and business models to business activities and every activity of the organization and the wider ecosystem in which it operates. It is the butterfly effect in action. Think about how practically all business processes are linked together, how businesses are connected from the customer's point of view, how information is transmitted through all digital transformations, what effects events can have on an economy, and much more. Here, scenario planning is important.

Because a holistic picture of digital transformation is important

While we only divide a few aspects of digital (corporate) transformation, it is of utmost importance to maintain this holistic framework.

Companies have always changed, and innovated, and technologies have always been associated with challenges, and opportunities, regulations, and ecosystems have always evolved. This is not new.

In the degree of connectivity and in the various accelerations that require profound changes at the corporate level, digital (corporate) transformation is more than a mere slogan. Nevertheless, in a fast-changing environment where the pace of change affects a wide range of phenomena, from the acceleration of technological advances and interruptions that threaten the status quo of current business models to the need for the pace to manage, the threaten, intensity and particularly a chance for businesses to achieve their core skills need to be successful.

Speak the same language

To ensure that we speak the same language, it is important to emphasize that digital transformation is not just about:

- Digital marketing, although this is an important part of commercial activities and the context in which digital transformation is frequently used.
- Digital customer behavior, although it is important, and customers are increasingly "digital and mobile."
- Technology outages, since outages are always customers, employees, markets, competitors, and interest groups, even if they are connected to technological developments and know that "emerging" technologies can have a "disruptive" effect.

- Converting paper into digital information, as it originally intended, nor digitizing information (flows) and business processes, which is simply an essential requirement.

We would rather talk about accelerated business transformation or digital business transformation when needed. It is only a matter of time before no one distinguishes between digital and physical or offline and online. For example, customers do not think in these terms or in terms of the channels.

Digital transformation and usual suspects: attention to advertising

Digital transformation does not only include technology but certainly not businesses in the technology sector or the startup scene. This is a typical error that can be halfway clarified why such "normal suspects" use "troublesome" computerized advances to change existing models and showcases, and - at any rate similarly significant: it pulls in a great deal of consideration.

Nonetheless, it is a mistake to find all these technology firms as examples of digital products that we continue to show. While some were really "distracting" because they forced older players to adapt or die, and we can learn from these startups and the technological success stories everyone is talking about, it's easy to overestimate them, certainly compared to the organizations that do have success in digital transformation in "less sexy" areas but at times much more stimulating and interesting.

The media and technology fans' attention to disruptors such as Uber and other usual suspects is not without its dangers and hype. The leading digital transformation companies are found in almost all sectors and are often not among the favorites of those who are fascinated by digital technologies and companies as such. The digital transformation is independent of the sector and begins with the company's objectives, challenges, customers, and the context of the company.

Even established companies are changing, if not all and at different speeds, and partnerships between established companies and "disruptive" newcomers are being transformed in different sectors such as the financial sector. Finally, these so-called disruptive companies can and will be affected by any growth. Your success is not guaranteed for pure long-term and digital players who satisfy the human need for human interaction sooner or later.

Myths and realities of digital transformation

Digital transformation is on the radar in many companies. To achieve similar benefits, it is important to focus on real business and customer challenges, follow a clear, often organized approach to prioritize all stakeholders, and engage them in every digital transformation process.

The following Capgemini chart (see the Capgemini eBook: "The digital advantage: how digital market leaders outperform their colleagues in every sector") dispels some myths and offers some realities.

Four realities of digital transformation that we want to highlight:

1. The relationship between business and IT is fundamental (bridging the gap between the two,

focusing on the same objectives and DO NOT neglect the role of IT).

2. Digital leaders have common DNA, and the road to digital transformation has common features (even if the context is important).

3. As I said, every sector is affected, including your sector. Customers, employees, partners, competitors, or disruptive new players are waiting for the business to reach regardless of the sector.

4. The digital transformation is managed from the top (or at least requires a fixed buy-in from the top - and by all those involved, if it wants to be successful throughout the company, this happens from the bottom towards the above and from within the projects). It is often the CEO, the Chief Digital Officer, or the CIO, but depending on who you ask, the CMO is also mentioned from time to time.

The transition from transformation technology to the transformation economy in 5 steps

Despite the above limitations on technology and IT, a secure link with new technologies exists. Let us, therefore, look at how this so-called digital economy is evolving.

Level 1: the third platform and digital business

In 2007 IDC launched the third platform, which was made up of four technological / business pillars: cloud, big data/analysis, social (business), and mobility.

Gartner called it the "Nexus of Forces" and spoke like others on SMAC (social, mobile, analytics and cloud). Regardless of the name, the critical point was that these technologies, and above all their acceptance by consumers, employees, and companies, their behavior-changing effects and the way they have been used to achieve various objectives, have radically changed reality corporate - a digital business reality.

Level 2: the innovation accelerators of the third platform

Various other technologies have been added to the third platform, preceding the era/platform of the mainframe or client-server model, which IDC has called innovation accelerators.

This includes robotics, natural interfaces, 3D printing, the Internet of Things, cognitive systems, and next-generation security. So we are still at a predominantly technological level here, but we are more focused on business and customer innovations (in addition to traditional optimization goals, etc.).

Level 3: from digital transformation to the level of innovation

What we see now, at least for companies that have implemented initiatives with a definite maturity in different areas and a longer-term vision, is that innovations (in terms of new business models, customer loyalty opportunities, construction of ecosystems with new entries, etc.) Essential because the foundations, objectives, strategy, culture, and vision are there.

The technology, creativity, and the use of the Digital Kunden experience lead us to this famous next wave of digital transformation developments, or an extra degree of innovation, thanks to digital learning, innovation, competitiveness, differentiation, automation, reductions in costs, efficiency, speed, and knowledge. In turn, this led to an innovation phase, according to IDC, and information is essential to make it possible. In an end-to-end approach, digital transformation requires excellence in IT and knowledge.

Level 4: accelerate innovation and transformation

This level of innovation and other challenges posed by disruptive business models will accelerate in the coming years.

In other words, we will see (we will see) change the pace of innovation and transformation and lead to a phase in which the disruptive effects of digital transformation can be felt in every sector as companies change switches and massively increase their mass. Digital transformation, as IDC's Frank Gens states, ensures a leadership role in the "digital industrial revolution."

Level 5: digital transformation at the center of a new economy

After all, IDC calls the digital transformation economy or DX economy to place digital transformation at the core of growth and innovation strategies.

You're going to hit these markets more quickly and quickly than ever. Moreover, accelerators of technologies such as the Internet of Things, cognitive (artificial intelligence), and the like will be the key for this growth, as will those "ordinary" backbones on the third platform (cloud, big data/analytics, web, etc.).

Accelerate innovation and transformation

While a variety of technologies have accelerated disruptions, business innovations, and changes in human behavior, exponential growth and the pace of change are only a fraction of what is yet to come.

Although the transformation of the digital business does not concern digital technologies as such, it is clear that the acceptance and possibilities of the techniques are sponsored by a charitable company, cloud, mobility, big data (analysis), cognitive computing and the Internet of Things and always the more society will change.

However, the current acceleration occurs when the acceleration of innovation and transformation, as such, is exponential. And that's precisely what analysis means when they talk about the digital transformation or the DX economy: accelerating the interruptions and changes and accelerating the current digital transformations and innovations that the leading companies are going through widening the gap. Latecomers become even more significant.

Digital transformation and intelligent information

In the context of digital transformation, the management of information and data is fundamental, but not sufficient. In the information and data business of today and tomorrow, insights, news, and measures are the most important: the results.

This is where context, semantics, artificial intelligence, and activation come into play. The Internet of Things and Web 3.0 is becoming more and more important to the comprehension and the use of knowledge in the workplace, unstructured knowledge, automation, and mobile devices. That's why we talk about "intelligent information activation."

On the way to information-based organizations and information that has become part of corporate capital and corporate resources, an intelligent information management approach is introduced into the boardroom.

At the same time, activities and data value are viewed from the perspective of commitment, results, and last mile.

This uses data, brings devices (IoT) into an ever more complex and that data landscape; it is important that unstructured data is steeply created, meaning and knowledge are extracted from information and used in good time for the right reasons and behavior.

From information management to intelligent information activation

The control of information in the conventional sense is no longer the only problem. It is not just a question of connecting or connecting systems and data through information. When the Internet of Things comes in, various factors complement the knowledge and transformation equation in the need to ensure data quality and the growing need to use and access them quicker, given the enormous number.

Among these are:
- Intelligence (as with artificial intelligence as the only way to add and extract meaning from an increasing number of data and the only way to use information and data in an IoT context and between devices).
- Speed (where speed is a customer experience and even a competitive advantage)
- a holistic approach to security (with information and data as resources),
- the need to digitize and acquire paper data (digital transformation requires digitization and therefore scanning), closer to the source, owner and process to become paperless (paper slows down digital transformation);
- and a growing focus on accuracy, quality, and results.

What does all this mean, and how will it develop? In addition to the existence of recording systems and involvement systems, both necessary, we move towards intelligent intelligence and automation systems and optimization, towards code ecosystems, algorithms, cognitive computing (understanding and beyond) and fast/smart Data as a means for success in digital transformation and, conversely, information-based challenges as the engine of transformation.

TECHNICAL EQUIPMENT: WEBSITE, APP AND VIRTUAL PLATFORMS

Virtual Events In 2020: The Definitive Guide

The value of personal interaction will never disappear, but sometimes it is a necessary part of the event's program to become virtual. But how does a multi-day conference with networking opportunities, training sessions, and insights acquired by the participants turn into virtual events?

And how do you ensure that waiting times are activated during the event?

The management of a virtual event needs the same focus. In any case, the case must be successfully advertised, participants involved, memorable waiting times generated, and the success of the event demonstrated.

The only thing missing is the place and presence on the spot. However, if you think of virtual events not as small single presentations, but as value-added and engagement-oriented experiences, you can create a live event that goes far beyond a computer screen.

What is a virtual event?

You may have attended an online webinar, participated at an on-demand training course, or attended a meeting using a video conferencing tool. You may also have participated in a conference from the comfort of your desk. Both of these are virtual event instances. A simulated event is an event where people experience the event and its contents online and not directly.

Four main types of virtual events

When it comes to the entire event program, you can add virtual events to the mix of hosted events, the events visited, and the internal events. Virtual events do not replace other types of events, but a new model to add and improve the whole program. The main four types of virtual events are listed below.

1. Webinar

Webinars usually last between 45 and 80 minutes. By holding webinars, participants from all over the world can participate and listen virtually while presenters present the content. Companies can charge for participation in the webinar through online payment services or offer it for free. Webinars generally use video conferencing tools that allow questions and answers, the opportunity to present life, or a recorded video and are subsequently offered as a tool on request. Due to their unique educational nature, webinars have been successful with 100% virtual participation. This may also include internal and external training.

2. Virtual conferences

Like personal conferences, virtual conferences are based on a complex live agenda that includes keynotes, meetings, explosions, and more. Virtual conferences contain multi-session content and may consist of community engagement tools. Although virtual conferences are not as effective in acquiring contracts and networking as a face-to-face event, they allow participants to view keynotes in real-time, create their plan from relevant content on-demand, and interact with other participants.

3. Internal hybrid events

These are town halls, sales launches, company-level events, training courses, departmental meetings, and more. For organizations crossing countries or even continents, internal hybrid events are used to send a message to the entire company if not all employees are gathered in the same place. Although it would be fantastic to fly all employees to your company's headquarters, it would be incredibly expensive, and the planning required would be time-consuming. The next best option is to host partly personal, partly virtual events.

4. Hybrid external events

These events take place outside of this organization. You may attend conferences or workshops in the industry. Such events require a higher video production level so that practically waiting times are equivalent in quality to individual waiting times. These events allow people who are unable to travel to the event to participate and learn. Offering the same value to external hybrid events is a challenge. Personal waiting times can be connected more freely online and interact with content more quickly than those who participate virtually.

Why host a virtual event?

For the same purposes as your activities, virtual events take place: relay the message to you, increase your client profits and profit, increase popularity, and increase lifelong loyalty. Meeting planners and event organizers have chosen between intimate, virtual, and hybrid events for years, and every form of the event has its advantages and disadvantages. For example, the webinar benefits from being virtual, as it is specifically designed to form an extensive network to provide thought leadership, training, or other content. In contrast, a user conference or regional training program is designed to create 1: 1 Customs conferences are designed - personal interactions that have improved face to face. When deciding whether your event should be planned virtually or not, consider what you can expect from the event and how well these goals can be achieved virtually compared to personal goals.

Here are some reasons to host a virtual event:

- Accessibility: while the event is still taking place in person, you can use the virtual options to take into account the waiting times in which you cannot participate personally.
- Budget: your business must cut costs and virtualize small events and webinars to raise funds for the year's biggest event that earns the most leads. It is also useful to have a virtual or hybrid option if waiting for budgets is a problem.
- No other option exists: no matter whether the weather conditions are severe, travel ban, or God's actions, you must schedule or cancel your case.

In-person or Virtual - The Fundamentals Matter

The basics are essential when planning events. All personal or virtual events are probably already part of your integrated marketing mix. Do you think holistically about your private and virtual events? Think about it. Your customers and potential participants will take part in both your personal and virtual events. They all work with the rest of your marketing mix to reach your audience and give you a complete picture of interest. Therefore, virtual events should not be separated from the rest of the events. They must be integrated into the meeting and event program.

Basics of event planning

- Virtual events such as personal events require good marketing. Participation suffers without targeted and useful advertising.
- Content is king. In a virtual environment, your content is your event. Powerful keynotes and engaging sessions tailored to the participants are essential.
- Alone doesn't have to mean just. Keep your virtual waiting times busy. Offer options relevant to each type of participant and use the online event guides for virtual events.
- Data is the only way to demonstrate the success of an event. Measuring engagement and recording waiting times and dates are the only

way to show the ROI of an event and activate the buyer's journey.

However, personal and virtual events are not the same

Virtual events have limitations that do not exist in individual events. Where different events with a single goal and the promise of networking can be delayed, virtual events must be content-based. In those segments which receive the best response, marketing experts and designers have to market content. So planners have to consider whether to provide material for virtual events. Break-outs and several content choices are conducted simultaneously for personal events. Do you expect to organize a virtual event that also needs to provide different content options simultaneously? It has to be given a decision. It is even more challenging to attend virtual meetings and require innovation and technology to impact events like mobile event applications.

Another reality is that personal commitment suffers in virtual events. There is no way around it. Networking from one participant to another is not as practical, and sales meetings must be held retrospectively, using the data collected virtually rather than the leads received on site. If you make your conference virtual, you can still create this 1: 1 meeting with your sales representative to discuss the account specifications in the following days. After the event, post-event tracking must be faster. Data is critical, and monitoring must be fast and accurate. Virtual events can never offer the same level of personal interaction as personal events. Besides that, there are ways to make virtual events successful, but it requires careful planning, excellent data, and flexibility.

Virtual event items

A virtual event is focused on content, data, and participation. Although F&B is not needed for virtual events, it is composed of many of the same elements as any other event. Video production quality and accessibility are essential as well as the website on which the software and the videos are stored. Here are the components of a simulated event:

- Website of the event
- Registration of the event

- Content of the live presentation
- Live audio/video in one direction
- Question and answer
- Live survey
- Take favorite notes/slides
- Recorded content
- Interactive video conference
- Feedback surveys

A platform for event technology and virtual events to host a virtual event

Virtual events are based on technology. Participation would not be possible without the use of computers and mobile devices. However, virtual event technology offers much more than just video conferencing tools. Like a personal event, virtual events benefit from the use of a comprehensive event technology platform that you can use to promote, run, and manage your event. The following are the key elements of event technology that you can use to run your virtual event.

Event Website

The event website will be used to promote the event. It has the same purpose, regardless of whether the event is virtual or personal. The event website is the most important advertising medium to interest potential prospects and gets them to register for the event. The event website must communicate the value of the virtual event, including the event schedule, present speakers, include frequently asked questions, and contain potential registration points.

Registration

Registration is the first data collection tool and is crucial to the case. You can register for virtual events, submit settings and personal information, and make payments as necessary. Registration systems allow you. A robust online registration tool simplifies the registration of registrants. It provides planners and marketing experts with the data they need to plan a big event and demonstrate the success of an event.

E-mail

E-mail marketing will boost demand for an event and increase registration numbers, update wait times before the event, allow waiting times before the virtual event, and eventually use feedback surveys. E-mail is the perfect way for participants to connect at all levels of the event. Using a tool for e-mail marketing to send tailored and personalized e-mails, to optimize the time when e-mails are received and delivered as planned.

Online event guide and mobile event app

The online event guide and the mobile event app, one of the most critical event technologies for virtual events, are the basis for waiting times. You may be shocked, but for personal and virtual events, mobile event apps are critical. Such applications run on mobile devices and web browsers and are the primary waiting times information source. Agendas with meeting ties generate material for the participants. You can choose which sessions to add to your schedule and where planners collect session popularity data and await engagement. These tools also connect the waiting times and provide messaging tools with which the waiting times can be virtually networked and connections promoted.

Event feedback

Event feedback is critical for virtual events when planners cannot judge responses based on the expressions or verbal feedback of people expected on the spot. Use event feedback tools to collect feedback through post-event surveys to help demonstrate the success of an event. Event feedback can also be used as a tool to qualify virtual leads and sell them.

Integrations

The integrations ensure the exchange of vital registration and waiting for data between your event technology system and your virtual event platform. This data can also be shared with your marketing automation and CRM systems. Use the integration tools to keep your waiting times and data in one place so you can jump on leads faster and analyze critical information from events such as meeting attendance and engagement.

Basics: how to host a virtual event

You have agreed to schedule a virtual event or want to do so. What's it like? The method of preparation is quite close to every other case. You can do the same for a simulated event, just as you will be able to prepare your actual situation. They wouldn't wait in their seats for more than two hours, and the same goes for virtual events. When planning, use standard planning tips and tricks to create and run a big event. Virtual events may seem different, but the more you treat them as a personal event, the better.

Questions when planning a virtual event
- Will the content be live, on-demand, or mixed?
- Have you created a pre-event waiting guide that explains how to attend keynotes, meetings, and how to use messaging tools?
- What are your KPIs for the event? While you may be less focused on the leads you've won, you can set session recording goals and feedback surveys.

- What happens if there is a connection problem?
- Will you charge a fee for your event, or will you offer free access?
- How long will sessions be available on-demand after the event?
- How long will the sessions last?
- What tools must participants have to create networks and schedule appointments?

Prepare participants for virtual events

When it comes to technology, a user error occurs. Virtual events aren't the same. Video conferencing tools and event development solutions are available in several different ways. Technical know-how (or lack thereof) should not be taken as a matter of course. Until the event, a guide to how to get to the case, sessions, and more are recommended. Practice waiting times even better to practice starting sessions or sending messages before the event starts. This simplifies, waiting for stress, reduces the flow of questions for a drip on the first day of the event, and offers an overall better experience. This guide should not be obsolete. Will your event have a sort of host? Let them record an introductory video that teaches them by adding humor to the content.

Participation in virtual events

Personal events are designed for engagement. From the network to happy hour to individual appointments for live questions and answers, these events involve the participants instead of leaving them sitting for hours and listening to the contents. You may think that virtual events are not an opportunity to get involved - you would be wrong. Keynotes, although viewed individually, can use live surveys to meet expectations. Sessions can still include live questions and answers. Commitment resources in the form of event technologies remain available. Messages in a mobile app allow participants to meet and hold meetings remotely. As always, social media is an excellent tool for leveraging engagement. When you use a hashtag for an event and Attendee publishes photos of the day's favorite takeaways, office configurations, and more, Attendee feels part of a community.

Networking and connection during virtual events

Just because a virtual event can't shake hands doesn't mean there is no way to connect to it. A mobile event app, used on the phone or in a web browser, can connect and provide a messaging system. As soon as the connection is waiting in the app, you can organize individual appointments with each other, with exhibitors or sponsors. Consider providing dedicated network time to encourage waiting times. Using the registration data, Link waits with similar interests and sets up group chats and outbreaks. Facilitates networking with video calls, chat groups, and appointments.

Data from virtual events

The data available varies from personal events to virtual events. Data will continue to be collected before, during, and after the event. They can be used to qualify leads, demonstrate the event's success, and improve the event for the following year.

Data collected during virtual events
Number of registrations

- Demographic information about the subscriber
- Recording of the session
- E-mail opening and click-through rate
- Post-event survey results
- Number of leads
- Interest in the purchase
- Evaluations of the session
- Feedback on the session
- Involvement and reach of social media

Demonstrate the success of a virtual event

Success in a simulated event relies upon the harmonization of the event and the organizational goals. Essential performance metrics are defined to assess the progress of the event before the event. Evidence of event ROI requires cost and benefit analysis. The prices are expressed as direct costs, indirect costs, and opportunity costs. The benefits include direct revenue, assigned revenue, assigned sales pipeline, brand value, and knowledge sharing. Using the data collected from virtual events to evaluate costs and benefits, you can demonstrate the success of your event. Formulate event metrics before the event starts. After the event, take the time to use your measurement data to understand if the event was successful and how you can improve.

How to turn your last minute live event into a virtual event

You can need to take a short turn and cancel the case or make it interactive. It's not so challenging to virtualize an example if you have the right infrastructure. It takes effort to arrange travel, lodging, F&B, and other items, but transferring material from personal to virtual is not as complicated as you would imagine.

Questions to pose before switching to a virtual event
- Can your plan be translated into a virtual environment, or is a personal event required?
- How will you follow the participation?
- Does your company have a solution to virtual meetings?

- Does the organization's personnel help and handle the technological aspects of a simulated event?
- Can you manage bandwidth?
- Do your participants have all the material they need for virtual participation?

How to plan a virtual event
- Update the website of the event and wait by e-mail to let the event know that the event is becoming virtual and the reason for the change
- Give waiting for people instructions on how to participate in the event virtually
- Add links to the session record or live broadcast on the list

Virtual events as part of the meeting and event schedule
Finally, it is good to add virtual events to the meeting and event program as an essential digital strategy. Although we know that virtual events don't offer the same performance as personal interactions,

circumstances can make it virtual, sometimes very short-term. Suppose you have the right preparation and technology. In that case, you can trust and trust a pin for digital technology to provide you with an immersive and informative experience waiting for you to work hard on this target.

INCREDIBLE TECHNICAL TOOLS FOR BEST VIRTUAL MEETINGS

The technology keeps all the participants on the same page, allowing them to stay in touch and be part of the conversation or troubleshooting. Without technology, your event is just a call or maybe a smoke signal.

To choose the right meeting technology, you want to do the following:

- Cost-efficient. While some of us want to be cheap or free, the main goal here is that technology offers value for your group and is worth it. There are free (or almost free) options in many situations, but if they aren't, it's important to understand when it's worth it.
- Easy to use. Nobody wants to spend the whole virtual meeting to understand how to use technology.
- A single solution that is consistent with multiple platforms. Avoid using different development tools to do the same, and pay for them. Provide an office solution allowing participants to access and approve another solution at another venue.

Virtual meeting technology is a broad topic, so we've broken it down into several types you could use.

VIRTUAL SESSION APP

Notable and popular virtual communication apps include:

FaceTime

Yes, you can also use this video communication app for companies. Apple has just announced that it will start group chats for up to 32 people with iOS12. The new FaceTime contains cards with the faces of the participants and highlights those who speak. Users may also manually pick which boxes they wish to highlight/see. Unfortunately, this app is for Ios users only.

Skype

This simple video chat software enables individuals or groups to communicate with each other without remote charges. The biggest advantage of using Skype is that most of the users are familiar with this online communication service and have a personal account.

However, there are major problems due to the need to distinguish sound and picture, and blockages and disconnections.

Hangout Meets

After its 2013 launch, Google Hangouts has come a long way. In 2017, Google launched a business-friendly version that focuses on business and video conferencing solutions called Hangouts Meet. The communication platform offers video chats and conferences for up to 50 participants and SMS. The app works on Android and iOS. Meet will soon be compatible with Polycom, Skype, Cisco, and many other third-party products. Meet is fully integrated into G Suite so that you can join a meeting directly through a calendar entry or e-mail. On the other hand, users need to have a G Suite account to invite others. The platform also lacks some business functionality from other software for more complex meetings.

Enlarge

The video zoom communication software offers many options for every budget. From a free plan to its commercial option, which starts at $ 19.99 per month per host, Zoom can handle up to 200 attendees with unlimited cloud storage (in its big business plans).

Advantages: the free option also allows up to 100 participants.

Cons: participants must download before they can join. The free version has a 40-minute limit for group meetings.

Accompany

With this free screen sharing and online meeting software, you can request a custom URL, customize the meeting background, and maintain administrative control over your account. If you need more options and more attendees, the software offers rate plans starting at USD 10 per month per user.

Advantages: the whiteboard function offers an attractive surface.

Cons: there are no notifications when someone joins the meeting.

GoToMeeting / GoToWebinar

This online meeting software is the long-standing option that has been chosen by many companies because it has long been offering video conferencing services. Offers a 14-day free trial. After that, plans start at $ 19 per month and are billed annually.

Pros: While rates exceed certain other choices, both plans are dependent upon the number of participants and offer unlimited meetings. Pros: And if you have several meetings with only a few participants each time, the expense can be worth it.

Cons: downloading can be problematic. There are no options to participate in the cloud.

Other virtual meeting software to check:
Freeconference call

This free teleconferencing and collaboration tool features screen sharing and drawing tools and public and private chats.

ClickMeeting

You may use the virtual meeting program of ClickMeeting, but some of its features are more applicable for webinars. It's more than letting one another see your squad.

AdobeConnect

Reliable virtual meeting tool that allows learning sessions for attendees, webinar features, and virtual room options.

Cisco WebEx meetings

WebEx meetings allow screen sharing, easy use of a mobile app and can accommodate up to 40,000 people.

Amazon Chime

Amazon Chime works with Alexa for work and offers video conferencing, online meetings, calls, and chats.

eZTalks Cloud Meeting

This video communication service offers features for screen sharing, instant messaging, and whiteboards.

VIRTUAL MEETING TECHNOLOGY

Several resources are available to make the most of the virtual meeting. The key choices, notes, and methods for interacting are:

Clarke.ai

Clarke participates in the virtual meeting as an additional participant and uses artificial intelligence to listen, record, and analyze it. Clarke then describes the call summary and subsequent steps. This means that participants can spend more time contributing to the conversation and less time taking notes. This is a paid tool. There is a seven-day free trial. After this period, it costs $ 15 per month for up to 5 hours of calls and $ 10 for every additional 5 hours.

Google Drive

Google Drive offers functions for documents, spreadsheets, presentations, and drawings. Files can be freely uploaded, downloaded, or shared with permission or a connection. Although Google Drive provides easy to use, editing online is difficult in real-time.

Relaxed

Slack is a communication platform for joining your team. It offers messaging app functions, customizable notifications, and can be integrated into many Office tools. Slack is one of the most reliable messaging tools available for employees and a great way to reduce the volume of e-mail sent between colleagues. However, it is expensive compared to most other options. Slack charges a price of $ 8 or $ 15 per month per person, although it is credited to employees who are not active this month.

Groan

Teams can easily collaborate with this Microsoft product. It is designed to help employees interact quickly and build on mutual work. You can invite different types of employees, e.g., employees and external customers. You can also join and create groups.

Some call it a corporate social network. Limited customization options are a problem.

LIVE STREAMING TOOLS
Run The World (RTW)
Run The World is a newcomer to the online event landscape. It would like to help organizers (organizations, podcasts, developers, experts, non-profit organizations, communities, and companies) organize online events such as conferences, fundraisers, workshops, chats, and Fire Meetups, etc. They offer plug-and-play models to help beginners organize their online events. The pricing structure differs from other tools: when hosting a paid event, they make tickets for you and generate 25% of your sales. If your event is free, a service fee will be charged to the participant.

Ivent
For virtual meetings, hybrid conferences, and webinars, iVent provides solutions. The software does not use any templates, and it can be completely personalized and

marketed. Thanks to their life and on-demand streaming platform, the organizers can transmit audio and video presentations in real-time HD quality.

INXPO

INXPO is a corporate video streaming platform whose goal is to create TV-style event experiences. The target audiences are advertisers, marketing firms, and event planners. They offer a range of online products such as live video streaming, webcasting apps, video portals, and virtual event platforms.

Speaker Engage

Speaker Engage is a platform for event management, including the care of speakers, sponsors and communities, a central content management system, and artificial intelligence workflow automation. Prices range from $ 3,995 per year for up to 2,000 contact records to $ 11,995 per year for up to 10,000 contact records.

WorkCast

WorkCast is an online presentation and event platform that can be used to deliver webinars, webcasts, or virtual events and is fully customizable. In addition to features for content delivery, it also offers features for event management, e.g., Detailed analyzes. WorkCast offers self-service event options, monitored or managed, depending on the control and flexibility desired by the organizer. The pricing structure is made up of 3 levels: Present + ($ 145 per month, expected up to 500), Manufacturer + ($ 495 per month, expected up to 5,000), and Enterprise (no fixed price - offer required, expected up to 50,000).

ubivent with meetyoo

Ubivent provides multimedia meetings, virtual conferences, video exhibits, and live streaming services. The website allows the public during live streaming sessions to question or discuss the subject with each other. The framework can be built or completely customized using templates.

UgoVirtual

UgoVirtual is a virtual solution platform for trade fairs, corporate meetings, and conferences. Replicate the on-site material and understanding. The software is versatile and highly configurable and can be used to host a single online event or to create a remote, on-site simulated version of an event. Participants can visit different places and participate in different activities, e.g., Keynote and live break-out, on-demand sessions, 1: 1 chat, social networks, peer collaboration, etc.

vFAIRS

Organizations may hold virtual work shows, online fairs, conferences, meetings, etc. through this virtual event platform. You can link to live webinars and digital content via chat tools (audio/video). Scalable and flexible. The software is open.

VIRTUAL NETWORK AND COOPERATION
Glisser

Glisser is a platform for audience retention and analysis for live events and training. You can share your presentation slides to expect real-time devices and use audience interaction (via questions and answers, surveys, social feeds, private notes) to improve the experience and provide analysis of events.

The key features of the tool are a 14-day free trial, without waiting for the numbers.

Microsoft team for companies

With Microsoft Teams, you can keep all your team's chats, meetings, files, and apps. Microsoft Teams is free and includes unlimited chat and search, video calls, personal and team file storage, and real-time collaboration with Office. This may be sufficient unless you want more advanced features like meeting recordings or management tools. In this scenario, you will need to access them as part of Office 365 (from $5 per month to $20 per month user).

NetworkTables

NetworkTables is a platform that promotes networking for virtual events, making it easier for those waiting to meet the right people and register for round tables, 1:1 meetings, and keynote sessions. The tool, for example, offers a stable seating solution that shows all the waiting times already present at a round table. During the keynotes or in-depth sessions, participants can check who has decided to participate and book their place. For a 1: 1 meeting, there are in-app video calls and AI matchmaking that show who is the best match. The software can be fully integrated into ticket issuing and video conferencing tools. No app downloads required.

Remo Conference

Remo Conference is a webinar and video platform for virtual networks. It allows personal involvement in real-time by creating virtual network rooms where those who are waiting can interact with each other. In the in-app chat, people can request or vote, and they can immediately respond to the question. Plans start at 50 dollars per month, with up to 50 participants per event (up to 1 hour and 15 minutes). There are also free 14-day test models.

Icebreaker Video

Icebreaker Video is currently only available as a private beta and is a platform that aims to build relationships before real events occur, building a long-term commitment. The first step is to put together people in a group chat and then make 1:1 video calls in real-time. In-app notifications will promote talks and wait until you engage in the actual event.

QiqoChat

QiqoChat is a collection of tools for communication and interaction between members online. The main tools allow you to connect with other professionals in the video break-out session in small groups. QiqoChat is based on groups called circles. People in a circle can connect via phone or video chat (using zoom) and schedule live events with audio and video break-out rooms. Screen sharing, whiteboards, and collaboration notes are available for each in-depth chart. The first 1000 minutes are free on QiqoChat.

PSAV

PSAV is a global event-production company that offers virtual networking and collaboration tools as well. ClickShare, for example, is a wireless presentation solution that encourages collaboration by optimizing efficiency in the meeting. With ClickShare, multiple presenters can share device content without problems with a single click. Likewise, their mobile event app allows networking among the audience of events.

Shareholder

The partner offers branded event apps for events, conferences, and trade shows. The app is fully customizable and offers various network functions, e.g., loadable and filterable waiting lists, recommendations for smart connections, shake and connect function, direct and group maintenance messages, meeting planning, and much more.

The partner works with a variety of events and organizations of various sizes.

AIDA

AIDA is a mobile app generator that uses a simple drag-and-drop interface that allows you to create white-colored event apps for meetings, conferences, exhibitions, fairs, etc. o employee retention apps.

You can choose from 80 features, including network options such as private messaging, video chat, forums, lead retrieval, meeting scheduling, etc.

The platform is free for up to 25 users. Costs are $ 499 per event for up to 250 users and $ 899 per event for up to 500 users.

CASCADING EFFECTS OF VIRTUAL SALES ON SALES OPERATIONS

Sales managers need to adjust when we enter the era of virtual sales, which is a "new normal" where sales:

- Mainly through remote or digital engagements or
- Much more balanced between virtual and personal interactions

Sales analysis, vendor skills, and land planning are three areas where virtual sales influence sales planning and design.

Sales Analysis

Analytical evaluations have become an integral part of the sales contribution to sales strategy and planning. Traditional descriptive metrics focus on describing what's going on, while diagnostic analysis explains why things happened, and predictive analysis suggests what can happen next.

Sales managers should prepare for new insights to improve sales planning and coaching by answering questions such as:

- How has sales performance changed as sellers become more involved in virtual sales commitments?
- Are sales struggles limited to specific sales teams, product lines, customer segments, etc.?
- What sales activities are connected with the success of virtual sales?

The capacity of the seller

Most sellers are struggling with travel restrictions or restrictions. In a June survey, 23% of CSOs reported plans to move the sales force into virtual sales roles permanently. 36% of CSOs are unsure of their plans. When sellers don't travel so much, their ability to other businesses increases.

If the seller's capacity is expanded, sales activities must include sales staff implementation strategies and their coverage - d. H. Check the number of accounts assigned to each seller. The reduction in tourism should allow for higher coverage rates, improve efficiency, and reduce the cost of sales.

Territory planning

The traditional approach to the design of sales territories has been to have geo-cluster sales accounts to limit sellers' travel burden. With vendors relying more on virtual sales, travel reduction may no longer be the main criterion for planning areas.

Instead of focusing on the geographic location, other criteria such as market opportunity, customer type, buyer preferences, etc. should be considered. - It can be used to improve area design and vendor assignments.

The rapid spread of virtual sales has surely surprised most of us. Now that it's here, most companies need to adjust their sales and delivery planning strategies accordingly. Sales activities should play an important role in development if they also adapt.

BUILD THE MARKETING LANDSCAPE

The digital marketing landscape

Digital marketing: the definitive guide for 2020

Digital marketing is complicated but particularly important when you work from home and the COVID-19 epidemic. Don't you agree with that?

That's why we've put together this digital marketing guide.

In the past, marketing was considered art, and today it is more of a science.

If you master both the artistic and scientific aspects of digital marketing, you will surely be successful.

How to create a digital marketing plan

In marketing planning, the marketing strategies with which the company can achieve its general strategic objectives are defined. It is the feel of a digital marketing campaign.

Summary:

The purpose of this section is to summarize the key objectives, goals, and recommendations. It guides the study and decision making of the board.

A digital marketing strategy involves the most critical aspect of segmenting your clients, so you know where to concentrate. It will also help you secure a strong return on your marketing investments. You can see three ways of segmenting the customers in this short video:

Analysis of the situation:

Each segment explains the target market and the role of the company, providing details about the industry, results, competition, and revenue. This includes:

- A description of the market defines the market and its key segments, customer needs, and the overall marketing environment.
- A product review
- A review of the competition
- A channel and sales review

- SWOT analysis: this section evaluates the main strengths, weaknesses, opportunities, and risks for the company and its products.

Objective and problems of digital marketing:
This section lists the key marketing objectives that the company intends to achieve in the next period and the key topics that could influence these objectives.

Digital marketing strategy:
It outlines the general logic with which the company wants to achieve its marketing objectives and specific target markets, positioning, and budgets. It also describes specific strategies for each element in the company's marketing mix.

Actions and tactics:
This section of the marketing plan describes how marketing strategies are implemented in specific actions, tactics, and programs, answering the following questions: What is being done? When will it be ready? Who is responsible? And how much is it?

Budgets:

Each segment outlines a detailed campaign strategy for the operations outlined above. This forms the foundation for promotion, including products, production, planning, personnel, and other operations.

KPIs and controls:

The final section lists the key indicators that can be used to monitor progress and management to review the global marketing plan's implementation and success.

How to organize your digital marketing department

Each company must design an organization or a marketing department capable of implementing its marketing strategies and plans. Here we will examine the different ways modern marketing departments and the marketing team can be organized.

The most common type of structure is the functional organization. In this facility, various digital marketing activities are managed by a specialist. For example, a social media manager is responsible for all social media activities and reports to the marketing manager. This functional marketing structure works on all products and regions.

Companies that sell across borders or internationally often use a geographic organization. Marketing professionals are assigned to specific geographic markets to establish themselves in an area, understand customers, and work with minimal travel times and costs.

Companies of different products or brands also establish a sales management campaign system. With this strategy, a product marketing manager develops and implements a comprehensive marketing strategy and program for a specific product or brand.

For companies that sell a product to many different types of markets and customers, a market or customer management structure may be the best. Advertisers in the market management systems establish specific marketing campaigns for particular markets or consumers. An example is VIP banking.

Throughout today's economic climate, the marketing agency has become an increasingly significant topic.

Many businesses assume that less emphasis on goods, labels, and territories is required in the market than customer engagement and management.

Effective digital marketing strategy elements:

To design, schedule, project size, and execute your campaign, we will provide you with the fundamental elements of an effective digital marketing program and provide you with a clear structure for owners and traders.

Digital presence:

The company's website could be the basis for digital marketing. It is the basis of all your online activities and offers your customers a central resource for finding information and connecting with your company. As more people interact with brands via smartphones and tablets, it is important to make sure that they offer a consistent and responsive experience on all devices.

Content development:

Companies must develop information content, whether in the form of blogs, e-books, infographics, white papers, or videos, to increase awareness and interest. The content must be broad, searchable, and specially designed to attract and engage the public.

SEM and SEO:
The art and the sciences of increasing the popularity of a website in search engines are search engine optimization. Several SEO approaches vary from digital research and on-site upgrades to the delivery of content and links. Secondly, search engine commercialization tools like Google AdWords and ads are important for awareness-raising.

E-mail marketing:
A strong strategy for digital marketing needs a strong strategy for mobile. E-mail marketing is one of the easiest ways to create a following with a product or service. You must build a database and efficiently use e-mail marketing if you want to create tips, translate them, and build a relationship with your customers.

Social Media:

Some of the most effective means of interacting for consumers is the social media network. It helps you build awareness and brand credibility. You will build trust and reputation and hold the deal up to date with your customers.

Conversion and measurement:

After all, to measure and improve the marketing results as far as possible, it is important to have a test and optimization strategy. You will take the time to check the metrics at every point to decide what has to be optimized, what succeeded, and where.

Main digital marketing metrics to track

It is important to know and continuously improve your marketing initiatives. Before we can optimize our campaigns, we need to be able to measure and manage them.

In this short video, you will find three things to keep in mind when starting your digital marketing campaigns:

Now we will show you the five most important digital marketing metrics you should follow.

The first important metric for digital marketing is total visits.

Your website should be the main focus for new or existing customers. However, you can also measure the total number of visits to each location relevant to your campaigns, e.g., landing pages or social channels. If you measure the total number of visits, you will get an overview of how your campaign generates traffic.

The second important metric for digital marketing is the conversion rate

Whether it's e-mail subscribers, e-book downloads, or a pure lead generation conversion, every campaign has a goal. When we understand how many people have visited our site, we need to determine what percentage of them did what we wanted them to do.

If your goal is to download a white paper and have had 1,000 visitors, and 100 of them did what you wanted (download an eBook, fill out a form, etc.), your conversion rate for that goal is 10%.

The third key metric for digital marketing is CPC (cost per conversion).

In the previous case, since 100 of 1,000 people converted and completed their goal, it is important to consider how much you have expended on these 100 conversions. Let us claim that for your effort, you have invested a total of $500. Get the total amount spent divided by the total number of conversions to get your campaign's cost per conversion.

Customer Acquisition Expense (CAC) is the fourth primary factor in digital marketing.

CAC is an incredibly significant and multi-faceted metric that can be found both online and offline. We looked at conversions in the previous example that could be any goal you want to achieve. CAC concentrates, however, on customers and the risk of recruiting customers.

Let's say you spent $ 10,000 on all your marketing initiatives, from social media and content to SEM, SEO, and e-mail. All these efforts have helped you attract 100 new customers. To determine the CAC, simply take the total amount spent on all the initiatives divided by the number of customers won through these initiatives. In this example, our CAC would be $ 100, which means that it costs us $ 100 in marketing costs to win a customer.

Client Lifetime Value (CLV) is the fifth primary indicator of digital marketing.

Lifetime Consumer Interest, or short-lived CLV, lets one appreciate typical customer's interest across life. There are many methods of estimating CLV according to the business model. However, the simple formula is: (Average order value - customer acquisition cost) x (Number of repeat sales) x (Average retention time)

For example, let's say you sell magazine subscriptions for $ 20 a month, and the average customer acquisition is $ 15, with the average customer subscription for three years. Our CLV formula would look like this ($ 20- $ 15) x (12 months) x (3 years) = $ 180.

The customer lifetime value is now displayed at the expense of customer acquisition. The ideal ratio between CLV or CAC is 3 to 1, and some companies like Salesforce use 5 to 1. If the CLV to CAC ratio is too low, your business is not sustainable, if it is too high, don't invest enough in it will win new customers.

In the digital marketing strategy, simple search engine optimization (SEO

Too complex and innovative digital marketing is to be limited to a few components. However, with limited budgets and resources, make sure your efforts and investments focus on these six main areas.

Search engines have two main roles: identifying and creating a directory of all web content and providing a ranking of the most relevant websites and content based on what they are looking for. Therefore, ensuring that your web properties are found by the people who need your services should be an integral part of your marketing plan.

In this lesson, we will show you how to be successful with SEO and give you some practical tips.

Indexing and accessibility

You may have the website in the world, but crawling and indexing it doesn't matter if the search engines can't access your website correctly. This applies to both search engines and human visitors. Pay attention to the following:

Titles: Create catchy headlines that spark reader interest.

Keywords: Select the keywords that will help people access your website and be relevant.

Links: Linking to high-quality websites that compliment what your website is about. It will encourage websites in your niche to connect to you too.

Quality: Try to publish unique and high-quality content. This requires users to access your website because they are unable to find content elsewhere easily.

Freshness: you need to add new content regularly

Website speed and performance

The acceleration and efficiency of your website are not only useful for the user experience, but also the search engines. Google punishes slow websites with lower rankings. So be sure to measure and improve your performance regularly. Here's how it's done:

Using Cloudflaze or other CDNs: content supply networks primarily copy the website into the cloud and distribute content to users from the closest server. This reduces waiting times but also protects your website from security gaps.

Optimize image sizes and formats: uploading rather small files is much faster. It is important to minimize the size of the image files while maintaining the best possible quality.

Check your code: make sure your website code is correct and W3C compliant. Browser errors can slow down page load times and make pages difficult for people and search engines to read

Optimize CSS and Javascript of the website: compile all your CSS and Javascript files in a single document and compress them to add them.

Search by keywords

As SEO continues to evolve, one thing remains, Keyword Research, here's how to do it right:

Make a list of significant and appropriate issues based on your business experience.

Attack some keywords or expressions, which you think should be entered on the topic

Conditions of a search linked. Healthy ways to get feedback from Google Keyword Calendar, events or AutoComplete

Check for the favorite keywords, d. H. Those that are relevant to your business cause significant traffic and may have moderate competition.

Building links

If we look at the web as a big city, connections are the roads that connect each side. Link building helps generate referral traffic, but it also creates credibility and authority for your website. Having you started, here are some important tips:

Internal link: make sure your pages are properly connected internally. Pages should be just one click away

Get links from government websites in your niche. Figure out where the authorities in your sector are linked and see whether you can contribute.

Social media: to see the posts from people more likely to post the posts, not from the ties themselves.

Connectable creation and distribution: you need a captivating story of your brand or a trending topic in your sector that is tailored to a specific target group.

Inbound and outbound digital marketing strategies

Is inbound marketing the art and science of making strangers to customers, and how does it work? We do this by producing content, distributing it online, bringing your customers back to your presence, and cultivating and building relationships.

The three most important tips for inbound marketing include:

Define your audience

it means understanding their main points, needs, objectives, and having a clear plan to deal with them in due course. When you understand your target market's essence and desire, you can create a step-by-step map of how foreigners become consumers.

Have a clear content strategy and distribution plan.
Know your target group. Now you need to create content tailored to your audience and have a plan on how to distribute it to reach it. Where does your audience live? Are you on Facebook, are you on LinkedIn or Twitter? Am I in your inbox? You can reach them in different ways, and online works well.

Maintain and build your relationships.
You have your audience, and you have your content and distribution plan. Now is the time to bring people from strangers to customers on the buyer's journey. It is important to understand that not all customers are ready for purchase. How do we get people on this path? Well, we are creating personalized content for the people they are exploring. Create personalized content for people who are actively evaluating options and create personalized content for people who are active leads

and ready to close. Now, most companies focus on hot leads, but if you do, ignore it.

Outgoing marketing is what people traditionally think of when they hear about advertising, and it is radio advertising, TV advertising, and print advertising. It is a technique to make your message accessible to as wide as possible the value of your product or service to persuade and convey it.

Here are three tips for running an outbound campaign effectively.

Communicate your competitive advantages.

Many advertisements try to become cleavers but do not communicate the essential elements required for advertising without deriving any value. Make sure to communicate three things in your ads. The first is exactly your offer. The second is why your audience should want it. The third point is how your audience responds and how they should receive and use your offer. When you sell something by price, include the prices in the ad. When you sell your service, you must communicate the benefits that the user will derive from it.

Attract and hold your audience's attention.
We are continuously being bombarded with commercials, and our interest is diminishing every day. As an advertiser, I'm less than 3seconds away from you, whether it's an advertisement or an e-mail in my inbox. Once you get my attention, you know better what to do with it. It is also a good idea before posting an ad. We should look at what is happening in the world, either online, on the radio, or in print. Look at your competitors' eyes on their advertisements and see which advertisements offer products and services similar to yours and how you can differentiate your messages and your positioning in your advertisements to highlight and keep my attention.

Test and optimize your ads.
Now that you have a limited budget, focus groups on your ads and other people's opinions can help you understand if your messages are delivered, if the costs

work and if your ad is getting the desired result. A cheaper and easier way to do this is "So what test." Place yourself in the audience role. Review your ad and wonder why I should be worried. If you don't pass this check and do not have a reaction, your ad failed, and you should hopefully tweak a few things and have a real effect.

In summary, we want to highlight the competitive advantages and communicate these essential messages. You want to attract the attention of your audience and never let yourself go. Finally, you want to test and optimize your advertising to make sure it is the best.

E-mail marketing strategies and tactics

E-mail marketing is typically one of the strongest and most effective components of a multinational digital marketing strategy. Below are a few useful tips and ideas to improve the ROI of your e-mail. You will use them today.

Best Practice # 1 - TEST, TEST, TEST

The easiest way to test the subject for any e-mail campaign. This is a good starting point. However, you can check all the following if you want to take your e-mail marketing to the next level:
- E-mail messages/content
- Layout and images
- Action requests and buttons
- Day of the week and daytime customization
- The landing page to which people are sent
- Target group
- Device reactivity

Best Practice No. 2 — Aim like a sniper

Too many marketers rely on their e-mail marketing strategy to "spray and pray." You send e-mails and hope for feedback to as many people as possible. The best marketers use e-mail like a rocket to deliver relevant, valuable, and engaging content to a highly targeted audience.

Best Practice # 3: become personal

Everything can be tailored to the recipient, from the contents of the subject lines to the e-mails themselves.

Best Practice No. 4 - Motivate and set up incentives
Use incentives to increase opening and click rates: if you include an incentive in the subject line, you can increase opening percentages by up to 50%. "Free shipping over $ 25" and "Get a free iPod with a demo" are examples of valid incentive-oriented topics. The same applies to buttons and requests for intervention.

Best Practice No. 5 - Keep it simple
E-mail readers have short attention spans. After opening the e-mail, you have less than 3 seconds to convince me to continue reading or visiting your landing page. So simplicity is the key. Don't fill your e-mails with too many messages or goals, and one is enough. The same goes for the layout of your e-mail. Simplify navigation and navigation.

Best Practice No. 6: make it mobile

In today's world, most e-mails are open on mobile and tablet devices. Are your e-mails designed to fit on different device screens? Responsive layouts have become a key factor in e-mail performance, and those who have not made the transition now suffer.

Best Practice No. 7 - Build a Pyramid

Structure your e-mails like a pyramid, focusing on important content in the upper body and support them below with a broad base of details. Key messages and the call to action must be above the fold where the user does not have to scroll down to view them, and each message must contain the key information that you want to share and respond to the five W's (who, what, where, when and why).

How to achieve your company social media results

Your company can link directly from products to challenges through social media with your customers, potential customers as well as brand ambassadors. A dedicated audience is one of the biggest advantages of a brand. Do you know how you can use social media to strengthen these relationships?

We will show you the most critical best practices for the effective implementation of the social media strategy:

Clarify your company's social media goals:

Clear targets are the most critical aspect of the social media marketing strategy. They affect your decision-making, and you have a slim and non-effective social media strategy without clearly specified goals. To order to prevent this, write for your business at least three social media targets. Ensure that every goal is precise, practical, and observable.

Find your audience:

Too often, we see brands involved in all social media channels to be present anywhere and everywhere. The first key to success in a social media initiative is how involved and active your audience is on a given network and can have the maximum impact. It is worth studying the relationship between social channels and your company to understand which business has the greatest impact on the desired results.

Develop your content strategy:

The previous two tips should now provide a framework for developing a global content strategy for your marketing plan. In the content strategy, you need to specify the type of content you want to publish, how often you publish the content, who the audience is, who creates the content, and how to advertise it.

Plan and use the program:

You can use pre-planned content to save time by preparing and carrying out the social media strategy. This helps build an audience and prevents you from flooding your follower feed with too much or too much information. By planning, you can maintain a steady stream of published content throughout the day. Another advantage of scheduling your posts is that you can continue sharing messages, updates, and content when you're busy or out of the office.

Use Analytics to track your progress and customize your strategy as needed:

Once you've implemented your social media marketing plan, it's time to review the metrics and see how your content behaves based on your goals. After analyzing your current campaign, you decide to do more about what works and rework the things that don't. You need to develop your strategy and content and use analytics to guide your next steps during your social media campaign.

Best practices for content marketers are an essential element of your digital marketing toolkit

Potential buyers and customers today get their information online from various sources. You and guide your purchasing decisions. Successful organizations are interested in the science of creating and distributing high-quality content to guide the buyer's journey. Easier said than done! Here are the basic requirements for a successful content marketing strategy:

1. Personas

Before creating content, we must first identify and profile our audience and the people we want to reach. But how do you do it?

Search your contact database to identify trends in how specific leads or customers find and consume your content

Use form fields that collect important personal information.

Consider feedback from your sales team on the leads they interact with most.

Interview customers and potential customers personally or by phone to find out what they like about your product or service. Plan the buyer's journey.

2. Map of the buyer's journey

It is important to identify the steps that potential customers or visitors take to become regular customers or users. Recognizing these steps is the key to creating relevant, valuable, and engaging content for everyone and at every stage of the buying cycle. In simple terms, different types of content are needed to create awareness, a separate set of content for the evaluation phase, and a final set of content for the decision phase, which means closing the deal.

3. Set content marketing goals and align them with business goals

How do you determine what should be produced and what should be shared with content planners? The material to which you conduct will specifically reflect your marketing efforts.

4. Create a plan for running and distributing content

Once you know the type of content you are going to create, you need to set up the process to create it. Your content execution plan should be a detailed overview of how an idea becomes a finished product and how this content is distributed

Various revenue generation models can be used to package, market, and sell products and services online and offline.

Sales of products and services:

Many online businesses and e-commerce platforms generate a good share of their sales. Supplements generate this revenue for products and services sold online. It is the simplest and most straightforward way to commercialize the deals.

Advertising revenue:
For publishers and online platforms that attract large or specific target markets, sale of online advertising space. This can be an important source of income. Advertisers pay to reach your audience if it meets their criteria.

Sponsorship income:
Platforms and brands can sponsor some or all of their content. In this way, sponsorship fees are increased to cover part or all of the costs. Whenever you see something "offered by a brand" that contains sponsored content.

Revenue from registration and maintenance (including SaaS models)
Signup paid for using their web site, or online marketers can also pay service. Many online publications, like the Wall Street Journal or the New York Times, charge their internet services for their subscription fees. These are

recurring payments in exchange for continuous access to a product or service.

User profile and data entries:
Websites and platforms on which databases with detailed user profiles have been created. Such data can be valuable for advertisers who are willing to pay to reach a specific audience. Facebook, for example, allows third parties to promote their users. These ads are based on several different criteria, including interest, geographic location, professional title, etc.

Transaction fees and commissions:
Those platforms charge fees for purchases between other parties exchanging on their websites' goods or services. eBay links buyers and sellers, for example, and takes a percentage of each transaction performance.

The recommendation proceeds:
Companies can generate revenue by referring customers to others. For example, hosting companies like GoDaddy pay third parties for every successful

customer they receive from them. This is essentially a tax for the seeker.

Connect the digital marketing plan a podcast

Why do you have to get a podcast?

You have the right competence if you have a passion for something or a subject. So you want to share it with others, why not share it with audio? A podcast is audio on demand. This way, people can hear what you have to say at any time of the day. You can run, drive, get stuck in traffic, or do exercises.

You can develop your podcast in a simple niche, a concentrated niche, and a downward niche if you want to establish your authority and reputation. You should target people near your target audience.

A mass group that follows you can be created. Do what you will do. Obey. Any area you want to think about. Within iTunes, there are 16 groups and hundreds. In any area, you want to talk about business, medicine, business. Let's say you have a career, you have many other subcategories, although you can talk about art, music and more. We only have 525 million subscribers in iTunes.

Why is it necessary to create a podcast? First of all, because you have a passion for something and want to share it with others. Two because you have and want to create your authority, and you want to be credible. And three, because the audience must only be yours.

WHAT IS CUSTOMER CENTRICITY IN A DIGITAL WORLD?

Customer orientation in the digital age

Artificial intelligence helps retailers to customize their offers, create personalized experiences, and make purchases more convenient.

Customer focus - putting your customers at the center of your strategy - has long been considered the holy grail of retail marketing.

In the digital age, customer attention revolves around intelligent data and technologies such as artificial intelligence (AI). With the help of artificial intelligence, companies collect as much data as possible about their customers' wishes, needs, and preferences and then apply them to adapt their offers, create personalized shopping experiences and make the purchasing process easier it's convenient. An example of new tools for understanding customer habits is the Personality Insight service, made possible by the IBM Watson artificial intelligence platform.

As we continue to see AI move from hype to effective implementation within organizations, retailers, and market players have new opportunities to gain a competitive advantage when it comes to customer focus. Here are three uses of how retailers use AI to transform their marketing strategies:

With AI, retailers can identify which customers are to be grown. A company's marketing efforts always run the risk of being ignored. There is a reason why John Wanamaker, the 19th-century pioneer of marketing, once joked: "Half the money I spend on advertising is wasted; the problem is that I don't know which half."

But AI helps companies know which customers are most receptive to their message - and equally important that they are not. Machine learning and deep learning with AI tools can analyze huge amounts of customer data in seconds. This helps companies distinguish between their most loyal and revenue-enhancing customers (high value) and those. The latter tend to buy products with the lowest or lowest margin (low value) and therefore develop targeted approaches for everyone.

Asos, the UK-based online retailer of fashion and cosmetics, uses a machine-learning algorithm to predict a customer's future value. The algorithm analyzes customer data, including information on a customer's demographics, purchase patterns, and return history, to determine its value. The algorithm then assigns each customer a "tag," which sends a signal to the online retailer. For example, Asos could promote high-quality customers by targeting them with more advertising or sales promotions and spending less time and marketing resources for low-value customers.

Artificial intelligence helps retailers provide advice on individual products. Chatbots, simple AI-based apps that interact with users via text, are some of the most popular forms of AI in retail marketing. Initially, companies viewed chatbots as cost savings: automating the conversations that normally require a human employee can save companies time and money.

Today chatbots are the main drivers of customer loyalty and loyalty. From the customer's point of view, the technology seems fluid. Chatbots mimic true human dialogue and offer user-specific content. From a reseller's perspective, chatbots can collect key customer information more efficiently than human representatives.

The best chatbots also make shopping fun. Sephora, the global beauty chain, illustrates this approach. Customers take an interactive quiz about their use of cosmetics, and the chatbot offers makeup tips and advice on individual products based on their responses. The chatbot then sends users to the Sephora website to complete their purchases. The company also has a bot with a virtual artist feature that allows shoppers to create a personalized look after uploading a selfie: a new approach that you should try before buying. This helps the business offer a more accurate image of a consumer's preferences and dislikes and forecast goods and services that might attract him.

THE FIVE BEST WAYS TO RECEIVE CUSTOMER FEEDBACK

Analysis and data provide us with all the possible information on our customers' wishes for our business. But sometimes, don't you want your customers to answer you directly?

This is customer feedback.

It helps us understand why people do something. Why do users three times higher than another use one feature? How will most of your customers stop in the last stage building accounts? Or what makes customers who use your product less often (and eventually stop using it)?

When we compare customer feedback with what we see in our analyzes, we get a clearer picture of what's going on. So we know how to solve problems and find the right options.

Here are the top 5 ways to get consistent (and high-quality) feedback from your customers:

1. Survey

Surveys are essential for getting feedback. They are easy to install, easy to ship, easy to analyze, and scale very well. What's wrong?

Two simple ways to manage surveys are available.
That one. Long analysis
It's best known to us. We can then connect to our list of clients, Twitter followers, and others after generating some questions with SurveyMonkey. Let's give it a few days, come back, and (hopefully) have all kinds of feedback.
Now many people get negative results when they send out surveys. Nobody finishes the survey, or the answers are not useful. It doesn't have to be that way. Use these simple tricks to make sure your surveys provide excellent answers.
Keep it short We have completed all the surveys that took over 20 minutes. Have you been 20 fun minutes that you like to remember? Of course not - it was a tedious job. And I bet you started reading the answers after the first questions, right? I do. So if we want to get high-quality answers from our customers, it is important

to ask only a few important questions. Try to limit your surveys to 5 questions and never go beyond 10.

Just ask the questions you will use. Each question should serve a purpose. And don't tell me that an additional question "could not hurt." It does. If you don't use the information you want, you're wasting your customers' time. You too waste yours. You have to go through a lot of answers, and none of them will make a difference. Instead, save time and get better answers by including only the essential questions.

Start with open questions. When you ask questions to your customers for the first time, you will be completely surprised by their answers. Therefore, when you create a survey with rating scales and multiple-choice questions, you limit the answers to your assumptions. However, if you use open questions, you know what your customers think.

ii. Short surveys on your website

The other choice is to guide your website to an inquiry. However, I advise you not to conduct a full survey directly with your visitors. If you want to publish a survey on your website, keep one or two questions that are highly relevant to the page where it is viewed. This way, you get much better feedback.

But how do we do it? Well, you should use Qualaroo. Create the question, select the page where you want to view it, and order the answers as soon as you receive them. This is a real question:

Qualaroo survey tool

This is a recent survey that we have conducted. As you can see, we are working on some improvements to our employee reports. And before we come to any conclusion, we want as much information from our customers as possible. And we are one way to do this Qualaroo survey.

Let's share this survey a little so we can see what's going on. Note that the survey asks two very specific questions. This is by design. If you ask vague questions, you will get vague answers. We are not asking if people like the relationship as a whole or how they want to improve it. We ask for feedback on a single function throughout the report. This way, we know if this part of the relationship needs to be corrected and in which direction we need to correct it.

We use Qualaroo a lot, and understanding how we can improve our product is an important part of our process. But be careful if you rely too heavily on surveys. If you only use surveys, you will never understand the deeper reasons for the answers you receive. I use surveys as a starting point.

2. Feedback boxes

Do you have a structured process to get feedback from your customers? Well, you should.

Your customers are constantly thinking about how your business could improve. Parts of your website may not provide you with exactly what you are looking for. Or maybe they found something that broke.

Most of the time, they won't reach your support team. This only happens if the problem is serious. But for the small annoyances and problems, your client will give up and easily leave frustrated. Surveys can identify the problem if you ask a question at the right time. But I wouldn't have expected it.

And if minor problems arise too often, customers will seek a better solution. So it's only a matter of time before they finally disappear.

How can we get customers to tell us the little things? Use a feedback form.

At the end of each page of our product you will find this form:

The purpose of this module is to make it easy for our users to tell us when something is not working properly. He is available as soon as someone needs them, out of the way when they don't need them, and sends his message to more people. It also collects information such as the account name, URL, and browser version to recreate the problem and determine exactly how to fix it.

I can only advise you to try something like this. Try different locations to find out which one gets the most feedback from your customers.

However, some websites have completely damaged the concept of the feedback form.

So far, so good, so sweet. It's vague and quick to use. Let's go ahead and click and get the following information:

If I were a real user and clicked on this feedback button, I would probably have gone from slightly irritated to frustrate. Because? Because all this form seems to work. I am asked questions about issues that do not interest me (do you want me to evaluate your layout?). Some of them can be confusing (what is a cache, and how can I clear it?). Instead of notifying Verizon of a problem, I now have to skip a few tires. After seeing this, I could be completely saved and never post the comment I have. The purpose of a feedback box is to get feedback from users on small things. This means that they have very little motivation to tell us about it. And you won't hear about the problem on other channels as it is only a small nuisance.

Make this feedback box as simple and intuitive as possible. Or you are missing the feedback it should capture.

Once the feedback arrives, what happens?

First of all, you have to answer. Yes, every last feedback gets an answer. And if you don't know what the user means. Here are some fantastic thoughts on how to answer:

When a user asks for a feature you want to publish, offer them access to it in advance to get more feedback from them.

ii. Link errors and technical issues directly to your support technicians.

iii. Ask for a detailed explanation (which will help you find the right solution) of what you want to achieve.

iv. Give them detailed instructions on how to use a different function in your product to achieve the same results.

Someone on your team should be responsible for responding to any feedback within a few days. Ideally, send responses within 24 hours.

3. Log indirectly

This is one of my favorites. It's one of the lowest ratings, too. If you ever want to understand them, you have to speak to them.

When we use surveys, e-mails, or analyzes, we lack all possible contextual information. Customers may say they need more money and more time. But what are you passionate about? Which one keeps you awake at night? You won't know exactly until you hear the passion in their voices when they talk about their problems.

You also want to be able to dig deeper. Suppose we run a SaaS business that allows freelancers to send invoices to their customers. And you recently received feedback (from surveys and the feedback form) that your customers want to customize their invoices. There are several reasons why you may want to do this:

that. Maybe they are designers and want another chance to demonstrate their skills.

ii. Or maybe your current design is simply horrible.

iii. You may want to change some important parts, e.g., adding footnotes.

Each of these reasons requires a completely different solution. If you don't contact your customers, you'll never know what's going on and try to solve the symptom instead of the real problem.

You will receive important bonus points if you do it personally. So dive into your client list and check if anyone is on the spot. Invite them to lunch and tell them you want to fully understand how your company is helping to solve their problem. Get more value from this one-hour lunch than from hundreds of customer surveys.

4. User activity from your analysis

Will, it is not nice to know what your website features and areas are currently used? And how often? Of course, we can use web analytics products to get an idea of the overall usage. But what does an individual use?

Most analytical products don't tell us what individuals do. This is because they are designed to track websites as a whole, not your customers.

However, if you are using customer analysis, you can view the activities of individuals.

What's the big deal Why is it useful

When we look at individuals' activities, it is much easier to identify why certain results occur. Let's see how it works in practice.

These are the data of a company that has a 30-day free trial. So the goal is to get someone to create an account and use the product, then demonstrate the value of the product so that the user wants to switch to a paid plan.

Since we received $ 0 in earnings from this person, we know they haven't switched to a paid plan. If we look at the timeline, we can see what actions they performed on which days (the bigger the point, but the more often they performed that day). It appears that they visited the site for the first time in early June and immediately created an account. Subsequently, they explored all possible functions on the website. But then the business subsided. Within a few weeks, this person never came back and never switched to a paid plan.

Based on this activity, we can assume that this person did not find enough value in the product offering and decided to continue.

With these data, we know who has NOT evaluated our business. And since we have their e-mails (they are blurred at the top), we can use some of these other feedback methods to understand better why they didn't think our product was valuable. We could contact them directly and try to organize a meeting. Or we draw a list of people with similar business models and send them a survey via e-mail. In any case, we already know exactly what questions we should ask.

5. Usability test

Maybe if you could watch anyone use your website or product? You can see the parts you're in, your focus, and where the frustration lies. This knowledge is of invaluable importance.

Okay, that's what utilities are doing. You may specify an operation that someone should execute, execute it by a random person, and document the entire procedure. Hundreds of thousands of dollars have long done it. You had to do something from a consulting firm by yourself. The rate is fair these days.

They are great for building new web apps and accounts. If you have created a new registration process or wish to publish a new product, I recommend looking at how someone uses it. This will immediately reveal some of the biggest problems and increase the speed with which you win new customers.

The bootstrap usability test

Let's say you boot and want to run some user tests on bare bones.

First, find someone who is part of your target market. So, if you sell to mom blogger, don't take a 20-year-old graphic designer (unless you happen to be mom blogger).

So bribe them with everything you can (maybe free lunch?) To try your new product. Put them in your office and ask them to do a simple task. Don't offer instructions or help. Watch them try to find out. Some of them immediately reveal the biggest bugs you need to fix.

But I don't do it with friends and relatives. They think you are big and everything you do is fantastic. So you cannot look at your product impartially. They reduce negative feedback and reinforce positive comments. This is exactly the opposite of what you need right now.

To get unbiased feedback that reflects what real users think, look for strangers for Bootstrap user tests.

When you need to make changes based on feedback
Now you get all kinds of feedback, which is great. But what are you doing?

If you have some degree of traction with your company or product, you will quickly be overwhelmed by the feedback. Between feedback e-mails, surveys, and user tests, you have many more ideas than you can ever edit. Regardless of what you do, you cannot respond to all the feedback you receive. You won't have the resources. And even if you had unlimited time and money to respond to any feedback, you wouldn't want it. That's because some of the tips you get come from nowhere - from customers who have tried to do something so obscure that personalization hinders the rest of your customers.

If you filter out all this feedback, look for trends. Let's say you see a problem this week, and someone else will see it again in 2 weeks. A month later, someone mentioned it again. And then there are three customers who all talk about it in the same week. This is the feedback you want to respond to. Talk to these people, get a complete picture of what they are trying to do, and then build something that makes it possible.

Bottom line

If you regularly collect feedback from your customers, you know if you are building your business in the right direction. So experiment with the methods mentioned above and find the right combination for your business. Once you find a process to collect high-quality feedback from your customers regularly, make it a standard practice.

DESCRIPTIONS OF IDEAL PEOPLE PARTICIPATING IN VIRTUAL SALES

Development Of A Powerful Virtual Sales Channel

Seven ways to improve the coverage, control, and cost-effectiveness of your sales channels

Virtual selling is now critical for growth in a market where distance selling is "almost normal" as the coronavirus pandemic has forced over 4 billion consumers, customers, employees, and sellers to stay home.

In a hurry to allow remote sales teams, the fact that virtual sales channels offer growth-oriented companies the potential to change sales performance and accelerate growth has been lost. Properly designed and equipped virtual sales channels can significantly improve the coverage, control, and cost-effectiveness of the business model, providing buyers with the speed and experience they need.

From a technological point of view, the pressure to adapt to this new purchasing reality will accelerate the adoption of existing but underutilized technologies that can multiply the seller's performance. This includes algorithmic sales, sales promotion, 5G communication, DTC channels, and even augmented reality.

From a business model point of view, virtual sales models are much more of a trend and certainly more than sales representatives when zooming. Your business can double customer engagement, productivity, and speed at a lower cost by offering seven key functions to remote sales teams.

VIRTUAL INFRASTRUCTURE - Tactically, sales managers must adequately equip their virtual workers with the basic infrastructure - unified communications, network access hardware, collaboration tools, and sales activation - must work effectively remotely.

Mo Katibeh, AT&T CMO, believes that the response to the coronavirus pandemic will lead to fundamental and lasting changes in the mix and composition of network traffic through corporate and consumer communication networks and the underlying infrastructure. "As in 2000 and similar disruptive events, the costs and complexity of relocating over 220 million employees, students and clients to homework will force companies and institutions to improve their communication infrastructure," said Katibeh. "Network performance is becoming more and more closely linked to employee performance as the economy becomes more virtual, and more customers are using digital and virtual channels. Moving to a more contemporary centralized communications network could lead to lower costs, significant bandwidth growth, greater flexibility, and the customer experience in the post-COVID era. "As a demonstration of this, the use of online collaboration tools for home and business has increased by 400% in the past three weeks, and video has been making more than half of mobile communications traffic, but according to the latest data, it represents more than 50% of the network bandwidth from AT&T network usage statistics.

In strategic terms, a virtual sales infrastructure offers B2B sellers the opportunity to differentiate the purchase path through video and virtual experiences that replace personal test drives, solution configuration, physical design, and visual experiences. A virtual infrastructure can also significantly expand sales coverage beyond the traditional boundaries of geographical, territorial, and functional constraints.

Saurabh Goorha, Wharton's senior fellow, chief product officer, the move to distance selling will force these companies to work harder to implement sales enablement, 5G communications, DTC channels, and even large-scale augmented reality. "At the tradition of creative product applications (such as travel and leisure), solely augmented reality technologies and AR / VR apps have been used but are increasingly important to the selling of consumer goods," notes Goorha. 'For example, eDesign services are utilized by architecture and interior design industries which allow vendors to carry out virtual internal consulting and 3D walk-ins spaces, including furniture and decorative facilities before they sell, leading to sales and higher satisfaction.

TRANSPARENT INFORMATION - The visibility of sales activity is a fundamental challenge in distance selling. It is not possible to manage what is possible to measure, and it is not possible to measure what is not seen.

Distance selling requires fast communication between members of the revenue team. A "horizontal" flow of information between sales, service, and product silos is particularly important for modern buyers.

For virtual channels to be effective, ways must be found to provide the entire sales team with fast, transparent, and complete information on all customer activities and commitments. This allows managers to delegate powers on the company's margins to support quick actions and decisions by remote sales representatives without giving up control and responsibility.

SALES CONDUCTED BY THE ALGORITHM - Advanced AI analysis and sales can better match the seller's time and multiply the seller's effectiveness by qualifying the opportunities based on the intentions of the buyer, giving priority to the accounts and recommending the right content, games, and promotions with the best chance of success. "It is clear that AI works in sales," said Leonard Lodish, a marketing professor at the Wharton School of Business. "The trick was to convince sales and marketing managers to try it and see it through long-term value creation. The move to virtual sales models will accelerate the adoption of sales artificial intelligence. Because sales managers have Difficulty Managing, measuring, and coaching remote salespeople who can't see or evaluating sales meetings they can't attend, it will force many companies to experiment more with advanced analytics to see how virtual vendors to measure, manage and improve. "

The perception of the use of AI in sales is very different from reality. The perception is that sales AI includes very complex and advanced applications, such as real-time speech analysis. In fact, from data and organizational maturity, these are not suitable for most companies. The reality is that commercial AI doesn't have to be developed to be effective in the short term. There is a large continuum of AI applications in the sales model, ranging from relatively simple to very complex. There are many effective and easy-to-implement AI sales applications that most companies can use today. Organizations significantly improve sales performance by using algorithms that support the basics of prioritizing and qualifying accounts and leads, recommending the content or promotion that leads to success, and reallocating sales resources to have the greatest impact. "

"In traditional personal sales interactions, non-verbal" losses "can interfere with the sales communication process, with a suboptimal impact for motivated sellers," said Goorha. "Digital settings allow the seller to display information about himself selectively. A phenomenon called the" motivational change effect "is triggered by the absence of typical non-verbal information such as movements or broken eye contact. "Which maximizes the credibility and effectiveness of their presentation in virtual sales channels."

SALES AUTOMATION - Any company can use sales enablement technology as a "force multiplier" to expand the seller's capacity by freeing up working hours first, thus ensuring a more reliable flow of customer retention and business information and finally taking advantage of the full potential of the sales technology stack.

Employees will save 10 to 30% of their time through the retention of clients by automating preparation, content discovery, and CRM reporting. In strategic terms, automation and sales activation can determine the return on existing sales resources, such as B. CRM - multiply by removing historical obstacles to realize their potential.

Bob Kelly, president of the sales management organization, points out that sales automation implementations like Sales AI don't have to be complex or progressive to be extremely effective and profitable in the short term. "Three decades after the advent of CRM, our research shows that most organizations' CRM implementations are characterized by unacceptable ROI, unsatisfactory user adoption, and a lot of unrealized potentials," said Kelly. "Sales automation can unlock this untapped value from CRM by removing key barriers to adoption, including simple data entry, pipeline management support, ease of use, and the creation of a single Salesforce information source."

Jeff McKittrick, Vice President of Sales Business Capabilities at Hitachi Vantara, agrees with Kelly's common sense. "In my experience, sales output and profitability can be more or more doubled by giving vendors the right resources, the right information, the right content at the correct time, and the right information to managers for their decisions. on resource allocation and best sales decisions are key performance indicators, "said McKittrick, who has more than 15 years of experience in implementing sales enablement and the digital sales platform." This dynamic, "continues McKittrick," has changed as the coronavirus pandemic is a turning point for the sales on virtual platforms to take full advantage of the automation value as sales teams need each minute to protect their consumer relations and respond to changing business opportunities and to improve customer loyalty in a toilet environment.

Virtual sales channels

PREPARED CHANNEL CONTENT - Virtual sellers must be faster and better able to find and recommend "channel ready" content that meets buyers' high expectations in terms of relevance, personalization, viewing, and collaboration remote environment. Digital salespeople should focus more on digital media and mobile networks, multimedia services, and teamwork to deliver what conventional dealers often need days and weeks in a few minutes or hours.

Personalized and engaging videos and even AR content are becoming increasingly important as online shoppers attach great importance to the content's quality and context. "The dynamic and interactive complexity of the knowledge needed to support new platforms provides more opportunities for increased inference and transfer, as it can be tailored more effectively to customer preferences and can be modeled in artificial intelligence and learning models on the market route diagram. "said Saurabh Goorha.

ENGAGEMENT METRICS - According to Steve Lucas, CEO of iCIMs, the most effective way to measure sales performance is for sales managers to develop a universal customer engagement quality factor that defines excellence of engaging stakeholders in the team's sale. Lucas recommends top management "as an organization to define the appearance of 10 out of 10 in terms of customer representation, quality of interaction, content sharing, and other related health data. Then use advanced analytics to create composite metrics with which the quality of customer loyalty at the customer and account level can be quantified and monitored. "

With available sales technology, sales managers can create metrics and incentives based on detailed data on customer engagement and seller activity. These provide quantifiable metrics for account content, quality of opportunities, potential, and seller's performance.

Measuring activity and engagement is useful for managers who cannot meet vendors in person. It is difficult to manage results, but it is possible to manage behaviors and activities. The linear cascading metrics do not exactly reflect the new purchasing reality and can be divisive, dysfunctional, and dependent on the game. Interdisciplinary roles and coverage model being, information, and advice. Jeff McKittrick points out that the lack of physical constraints allows you to extend your coverage beyond traditional geographical, territorial, and functional constraints and to use the best resources in the best place to drive a deal. "Competence within a sales organization is often isolated and generally unavailable or used by all teams," explains McKittrick. "In traditional sales models, these experts are accessed through inefficient methods such as e-mail lists and various messaging apps within a company. Unless the specialist asks the question, normally only a person who has posed the question is given a single database in which the entire organization can scan. Digital sales platforms can break through these walls using technologies that facilitate the exchange of information and offer an experience "similar to Google "for experts and information to find a specific context for a company's technology and solutions."

THE SELLER'S GUIDE: SUCCESSFUL ADVICE IN A VIRTUAL SALES WORLD

For many teams, the volume of business creation and responses to assignments have decreased. However, the data suggests that companies can attract and win potential customers in new ways. Website traffic, conversations initiated by buyers, and the opening rate of marketing e-mails are on the rise. Customers are still looking for involvement, but differently than before.

We discovered that virtual sales strategies must be adapted to reflect the current purchasing realty. Think about education, not advertising.

Mastering virtual sales mean focusing on potential experience during the sales cycle. With economic changes, it is more important than ever to measure the state of the pipeline and predict exactly where your quarter is going so you can focus your sales efforts. Here are five strategies your sales team can use to promote multiple connected sales and demo calls to be successful in a virtual sales environment.

Virtual sales, defined

Many sales professionals can fall into the trap of thinking and acting on what is important to them - their share, commissions, and needs - and not that of customers, especially in uncertain times like now. However, to establish human connections through the digital divide, it is necessary to think at each meeting level. For this reason, our list of virtual sales best practices starts with your settings and routines.

1. Set routines and spaces that promote focus

It can be an efficient way to optimize time from home. But it is easy to get away from it. Three ways can you build a working atmosphere in your home office.

- Separate. Dishes in the sink, children or pets playing, linens that call your name: the house can be quite distracting. Imagine that your desk is in the office. Try to find physical ways to focus better.
- Create and stick to a schedule. Too many of us slip into the bedside pit and work on our laptop before being told to be eaten by others. But this

is a sure way to run out. Start at a specific time, schedule meetings as usual (but with greater availability), and take breaks.

- Make sure you have all the remote selling tools. Additional monitors, webcams, microphones, etc. They help you create the right environment to maximize your productivity.

- Measure the conditions of your pipeline and reclassify them. This organizational step is digital. Difficult to live up to shifting expectations when your company is changed when you are split from your team. Focus your time optimally, and make it more productive with your manager, measure the conditions of your pipeline and reclassify accounts to highlight those requiring special attention.

2. Show potential customers and customers that you appreciate their time

Today is more critical than ever in time management. Although commuting interrupts work from home, many workers struggle to separate their work-life balance because work and life take place in the same place. Also, quick office chats have developed into zoom meetings that make it difficult for people to focus.

Allowing downtime between meetings is considered your customers and potential customers. Gestures like "I want to give you 10 minutes before the next meeting, so I want to cover these items before the call ends." By prioritizing concise meetings and putting their time first, you can stand out from the crowd. For example, you can change the length of the meetings as follows:

- 60 minutes → 50 minutes
- 30 minutes → 25 minutes

3. Videos and demos are more important

The presentation is important. You want to communicate professionalism and ensure that your customers and potential customers can see you as a thought leader. You want people to jump out of the sales field and say, "Wow, this team is extraordinarily good! It was the most effective use of my time and attention in an online meeting I've ever had."

Here are seven ways to do it.

Dress to amaze. You are tempted to sit at home all day in your pajamas. One routine that helped our team into the business environment, even if it only goes alive, is being clothed for work in the morning.

ii. Find a flattering light. Find a flattering light. The best light is available sitting in front of a mirror. If you can not, ask your company to provide you or both sides of the screen with lights you can put.

iii. Use the correct camera angle. The best choice is a camera just above the eye line. This will automatically tilt the head upwards. It is also more ergonomic.

iv. Take care of your eyes. Face in the mirror to establish eye contact with the future client as soon as possible. Turn off auto-zooming so you don't get tempted to look at yourself and position the participant's window as close to your camera as possible.

v. Select Do Not Disturb. Make sure popups and Slack notifications don't interrupt your conversations. Your client deserves your full attention.

Her. Stop sharing your screen whenever possible. Let's say you finished a demo and moved on to the question and answer list. Stop sharing your screen so that you can monitor your facial features and body language.

vii. Be creative with your presentations. For example, if zooming in on backgrounds, you can improve sales presentations and demos. Think like a meteorologist in front of a green screen: you can sequence backgrounds or record a demo as a background image to create a different type of visual interest and presentation style that stands out.

4. Preparation leads to extraordinary online meetings

Without the advantage of face-to-face meetings, it is more important than ever to consider how we can make the most of the time that our potential customers and customers make available to us. When you meet in person, speak naturally, and make more personal contacts. However, you are limited to a virtual meeting and want to consider what value you offer and what you want to achieve with this call. In this way, you can specifically use these options for deeper connections. Here are some tips for communicating before, during, and after the meeting:

Kick-off tips:

Thanks for participating and sincerely ask them how they are. It's tempting to start presenting directly via Zoom but to give meetings with Smalltalk a friendly atmosphere. Many people accustomed to the buzz of an office environment will appreciate the opportunity to chat.

Determine the purpose of the call and ask your guests to confirm their orientation at the beginning of each call. This is a particularly effective best practice for virtual sales as employees move from one digital meeting to the next. It is useful to repeat the topic and align everyone towards the objectives.

Meeting tips:

Try to limit the number of slides and screen sharing you use to prioritize the conversation. With a personal presentation, potential customers can look at you, the slides, and each other. You might just lose your concentration if you just stare at the slide on the projector.

Try engaging with them to communicate with others. Participants can retire at electronic meetings too quickly. Explore opportunities to engage in the questions independently.

Closing tips:

Say "Thank you! Making people feel appreciated is a long way. Especially now, when communication is digital, and we don't understand these real ways so often. Taking the time to show true gratitude makes a big impression.

Set up the next steps, such as setting up the next meeting, and send the next steps together with the documents mentioned in a follow-up e-mail. While this is always a good practice, it is important that your prospect cut off your call to the next - and the next, and so on. Setting up the next meeting right there and taking notes ensures that nothing slips through the cracks. When meetings are scheduled on the calendar, you and your executives can measure the state of the pipeline and accurately predict which accounts are on track.

5. Take breaks without feeling guilty

You are in a rut, turn off customer calls, reach your goals, and suddenly it's 17:00. You haven't had lunch yet, and you're stuck in the chair for 8 hours.

Studies show that breaks can significantly improve a person's level of productivity and concentration. Take a step back and give yourself a new space to breathe, go out, or train. It gives the brain time to recharge and relax. When in the office, you may have a desk standing up, get up for boardroom meetings, take a walk for coffee, and have lunch with colleagues. When you are at home, and all meetings are on the screen, it is more difficult to make up for that extra time outside the monitor.

Your mental health and wellbeing, particularly in times of stress, are significant. You can perform more and work more effectively by juggling your job and life.

MINDSET AND MOTIVATION

Do You Have An Attitude Towards Sales Growth?

Many in the sales community have been convinced that sales success depends on innate communication skills and a friendly personality. The assumption was that if you hadn't had "it," you wouldn't have learned it. However, a wave of scientific research examining what makes people successful has refuted this theory in recent decades. While some individuals are willing to develop into a stronger product, talent is not necessary. Since the extremely competitive market, your knowledge and expertise must be constantly developed. In other words, you have to sell outside your normal ability to be competitive in sales today.

A fascinating example of this is Carol Dweck, a psychology professor at Stanford University, who has conducted numerous studies on how one's mindset affects one's performance.

He found that people tend to have one of two common ideas.

1. Fixed mindset: you believe there is little you can do to change your skills

2. Sense of growth - believe that effort can improve your skills

Below is a quick quiz that you can use to determine which setting you have.

What assumptions do you consider to be true?

1. Your ability to sell is part of your personality, and it is not something you can change.

2. No matter how good you are in sales, you can always improve.

3. You can learn new sales strategies, but you cannot change your ability to influence others much.

4. Selling is an ability you can develop independently of your temperament or natural talent.

Questions 1 and 3 reflect arguments concerning the fixed thought, while the development thought is the subject of claims 2 and 4.

These mindsets will greatly influence sales results because the results of each product are radically different. Those who have a growth philosophy are far more successful than those who don't. One of the main reasons a growth philosophy leads to high performance is that it changes the brain's perception of failure. People with fixed attitudes tend to view failures as a judgment on themselves. If they fail, they feel failures. By contrast, people with a growth philosophy view failure as feedback that shows them how to adapt and take their skills to the next level.

Overall the years, I've seen the huge success gap between sellers who rely on their skills to produce adequate revenue (company's thinking) and those who work hard to develop their innate ability (Mindset growth) to meet or surpass their selling targets each year. In reality, sales managers need to look for this when they take an open selling role. Many with growth opportunities become more likely to excel and thus the best.

And you? If you have a growth philosophy, great! If you have a strong mindset, you should face it as this will hinder your ability to achieve the level of success you desire. The good news is that your mentality is your mentality, and you can change it. Choosing the new authorizing belief that your sales skills are like a muscle that needs to be constantly strengthened inspires the work ethic required to achieve a high level of sales performance.

SEVEN-TIME MANAGEMENT TIPS NEEDED FOR SALES REPS

"Time is time," as the old proverb states. No one knows the facts, more than professional sales staff. Every minute your sellers spend without engaging in high-profit sales activities means missed opportunities and lost revenue.

Successful sales involve manipulating many different businesses: some are boring and time-consuming, but simply cannot be avoided. This is where solid-time management comes in. It is a discipline that the most successful sellers master and integrate into their daily lives.

Share these seven time management tips for sales reps with your team to do more in less time before they know!

1. Eliminate unnecessary activities

Administrative tasks may be required, but they can increase rapidly and take a long time for the seller. If you want to maximize the sales time of your sales representatives with high profits, let them seek out administrative tasks that can eliminate, automate, or outsource. It may only take a few minutes here and there, but these saved moments can add up quickly.

First, check if it makes sense to turn over some of these activities to business development employees or administrative specialists.

2. Things happen; To be prepared

How do your sellers react when something goes wrong? The faster you can recover if a customer misses an appointment, goes bankrupt, or changes your product line, the more time he can spend on the core business.

This agility and ability to think quickly is an attribute to watch out for when hiring sellers. Hiccups cannot stop people who are naturally wired this way.

3. Be smart with e-mail

E-mail can be a very simple and effective sales tool, but it can also take a lot of time and energy. Your sales representatives can save a lot of hassle by having e-mail templates ready for repeated calls and organizing their inbox.

Train your sales representatives to configure the folders in their inbox to access information when needed quickly. In the meantime, read best practices for creating the perfect e-mail meeting invitation.

4. Multitasking is a myth

Your sellers will undoubtedly juggle multiple businesses on a given day. While this can make them feel truly productive, the truth is that the quality of work and attention to detail is likely to be affected. It takes time for our brain to switch from one activity to another, and losing concentration during this period can significantly affect productivity.

Employees can work on one task at once to produce optimum performance and obtain the required consumer interest.

5. Take the bitter pill

We all have a few tasks that we fear, and your sales representatives are no exception. Whether you are researching, writing follow-up e-mails, or filling out the activity log, there is a great temptation to postpone these activities. Encourage your employees to dive and perform them instead of putting off the inevitable.

Remind them that the sooner they are dealing with them, the faster they can move forward.

6. Use the momentum

After you have secured a contract, completed a significant task, or achieved a landmark, a break will reward you with your sellers' first instinct. Nevertheless, this seemingly innocuous activity is detrimental. It is easier to focus on our success and dive in another call instead of taking a break.

The moment is powerful and difficult to achieve. Sales staff should use the positive flow of energy and confidence to take advantage of another opportunity immediately.

7. Previous success replication

It makes no sense to start over in every new opportunity. Let your sales reps examine their won and lost opportunities to determine what has proven effective. They should be able to develop a kind of model in which they seek new perspectives, which questions need to be asked, which case studies are most relevant to a particular person, etc.

If one is true, sales success requires the ability to perform a variety of tasks every day. For sales staff to be successful and give customers and potential customers the right attention, time management must be prioritized.

These time management tips for sales reps are a good starting point for optimizing daily activities and gaining valuable time to focus on doing more business. As a sales manager, it's your job to provide your sales team with the tools they need to organize, create a plan, and stay focused.

COOPERATION WITH BUYERS

5 phases in the process of communicating with buyers

Either of two things must be correct when buyers buy something:

1. You have to buy it.

2. You want to buy it.

In the first, they have no choice. Get sued, hire a lawyer. Buy = required. The lawyer does not have to convince the buyer because he buys legal services in general, but only because he buys them from him.

The customer has an option in the above case. Buy = wanted. They don't have to buy, but if they want it badly enough and have the money and authority to buy it.

Since the buyer does not have to buy when sellers increase demand, sellers must prioritize sales and prioritize it for the buyer.

However, it's not that easy as you're not close to the buyer's priority list at the beginning.

The key to moving to the buyer's priority list is desire and ownership:

- Desire: you need to want what you can do for them.

- Possession: you have to take something that wasn't even on your radar screen and make her believe deeply, "I have to do something about it!"

Perhaps the most overlooked strategy for creating the buyer's desire and ownership is to involve them in the sales process by inviting them to collaborate.

Sellers who get the most sales work with buyers almost three times more often than sellers who occupy second place. Cooperation helps in almost any sales situation.

Cooperation in the sales process

Here are five steps to motivate buyers to work together:

1. Prepare buyers for collaboration: schedule a meeting that opens the door to collaboration. For example, you can set up the meeting based on the given premise to share ideas that you believe are valid for a buyer, but the ideas are not yet ready, and you need their help to think about them. This opens the door to their participation in the process.

Then start the meeting with the right presentations and expectations, including the invitation to immerse yourself with thoughts and questions.

If you involve buyers, the idea is to invite them to active participants in a process, not to someone who listens to a tone and then decides "up or down" when buying the sold product.

2. Asking the buyer: When sellers create their opportunities, they are often mistaken on the excessive launch. The seller stands up, hoping to inspire the buyer. The buyer isn't involved there, even if the ROI seems huge.

The problem is often not the impact the product or service can have on the buyer, but the psychological impact of insufficient participation in the discussion. Ask the buyer in advance to inquire about the possibilities with you. For example, you could say:

- This is how it happened in the other two locations of our customers. Imagine that you have implemented something like this for a minute, and the time will come in 6 months.

What impact do you think you can see? What would be the impact?

- You said that A and B were not issued to you, but C and D were. Only imagine C and D disappearing as a question for one minute. How do you see the impact? What 'd the result be?

- Which is why, by moving the marketing engine on all generators, we find it possible to boost revenue by 20 percent. However, we are aware that most business leaders, however much they wish to increase this type of sales, would be skeptical. Why shouldn't it work here? What would be the roadblocks?

Some sellers ask when they feel we are giving this advice, "Isn't it difficult to sell?" It is not so. The company is likely to want the improvements you think possible, but the risks are too high.

Let them talk about roadblocks, and you can talk to them. Leave the roadblocks hidden, and skepticism annoys and sales die. You won't understand why.

When shoppers answer your questions, you can share stories about how the problems they saw have been solved elsewhere. You can also ask them, "Let's take a look at the last block. How can we solve it?" Many buyers talk about problems while asking for solutions.

3. Ask Concise Questions: Once you have created the opportunity and asked for the meeting, it is up to you to set the table, set the tone and define the platform and agenda for discussion with the lawyers.
Nevertheless, that does not imply that at the outset of the selling phase, he has no serious questions which cause the purchaser to consider, which causes the buyer nervous and which summarizes the issues. Examples:

- Does doing nothing about this affect your productivity and morale?
- If you know you need to do something about it, why haven't you taken all the steps?
- You took action, and in the past, it has failed, but it looks like it is considering doing something like this again. Why will this time be different?
- If I have seen problems similar to yours like A, B, and C, it is usually a recipe for big problems like X, Y, and Z that arise at some point. But you

don't seem particularly worried. Could you clarify that X, Y, and Z will not appear here?

These questions are not a variant of the balloon. You're nervous. You will probably make the buyer uncomfortable. Well. If the buyer has good answers to your difficult questions, answers that make you think, "Okay, you don't need help," then it's fine for you. Now you can switch to other options. It's good for them because you helped them understand why they are already in great shape.

If they can't throw your difficult questions out of the park, help the buyer realize that the status quo isn't good enough. This means that action is needed.

4. Model the way forward: most of us don't just sell an offer. Many sellers have flexibility in terms of service or product package, delivery, and mix that they ultimately produce.

If the buyer helps model the solution, he will be proud of his property and commitment to consider it alive.

You could say, "We 'd be doing a, a, b, and c, because of what I've been thinking about, but I know we've got some unanswered concerns about some of the specifics. You said before that X might hamper execution." The customer might say: "It's sticky, okay.

The right thing to do in my experience is ... Be mindful, however, that the buyer is not told clearly if the criteria can be set without setting them: "What do you think we should do from here?" it's too open. They may have no idea what to do and may choose something that is not the best choice. It is usually best to give them insight into what you think is the best way and then allow them to shape it with you.

5. Assign ownership of the idea to the buyer: take the last point, for example. The buyer might say, "The best thing to do is this ..." You may already know, but don't say, "Yes, I thought about it during most meetings." When you do, you take the idea from them and claim it as yours. Instead, say, "I think it's a good idea. I bet it will work." In this way, allow them to retain ownership of the idea. Having the concept increases your desire to highlight it.

Work with your buyers in the sales process. Not only will they be included in their priority lists and planned action plans, but the likelihood that they will take these actions with you will skyrocket.

EFFECTIVE VIRTUAL NEGOTIATION

One of the areas that were moving to virtual can affect a company's ability to work effectively is through negotiation. How people or teams navigate and influence a situation to achieve the desired result, both internally and with customers or potential customers. As companies are more connected than ever, executives are likely to have to negotiate more and more practically where they did it face to face. Business leaders must become qualified virtual negotiators and pay attention to the negotiating skills they deserve when developing training programs for their organization.

When negotiations occur in channels where parties can see each other - such as telephone, e-mail, and video conferencing - the negotiating team's communication skills become critical and determine whether the interaction is successful or unsuccessful. In many cases, the same behavior of best practices in the real world is relevant for virtual negotiations. The same skills and techniques must be demonstrated: it is simply more important than they are exhibited in virtual trading environments.

For example, if it is not clear whether everyone is busy and sometimes pursuing complex interactions, an experienced negotiator needs to know when to summarize the discussion. This is important for personal interaction, but there may be a flipchart in the room where all the games are listed. While some virtual platforms offer this, not all of them do. This means that "we all agree that the project could start at a reduced price in March in the first three months if ..." is less a rhetorical recovery than an essential test to verify if real progress is being made. This means that "we all agree that the project could start at a reduced price in March in the first three months if ..." is less a rhetorical recovery than an essential test to verify if real progress is being made. The deal can be closed and when it's time to move on to the next item.

Frequently summarize your virtual deals

These summary statements are often more effective than questions in a virtual environment. The distinction is important because questions are important during a negotiation: they create doubts and doubts create movement. However, a steady stream of question marks in an e-mail forum or instant chat can be challenging. The use of summary statements - "so that we are all clear about the term of the contract" - instead of constant questions, can be an effective alternative.

Labeling can draw attention to virtual negotiations

"Labeling behavior" means marking what needs to be discussed in advance. "I like to outline our proposal," for example. It's worth doing it in every interaction. Still, in a virtual environment where you can't see the participants, you don't necessarily have all their attention, and you don't know if they are following the conversation, this plays an even more important role than the group's focus on what is being discussed.

An exception to this rule are times of controversy. "I disagree with you there" will cause people to shut down and ignore the reasons for your disagreement, especially in a virtual environment where there is less obligation to remain engaged. It is best to explain the reasons for a dedicated audience before highlighting any disagreements. "We offer a significant discount in the first six months, so we can't reduce the contract to just six months so that I won't agree with you on this," he says, without losing the listener in advance.

Prepare and plan a virtual negotiation

Understand and respond to the difference between preparation and planning - where preparation is the collection of facts, numbers, variables, and options; During planning, it is a careful choreography of topics, behaviors, and personalities that you will use as soon as you engage directly in the real world or the virtual space. Planning is much more important than both. Use some of the time you may have spent traveling to find out how to make the most of your knowledge of margins, facts, and figures in virtual negotiations

All of this means that companies don't have to rework the way they interact and negotiate internally and with potential customers, but they must be doubly sure that their teams are trained and able to demonstrate best practices. In these unprecedented times, effective negotiations must play an exceptional role for companies in almost all sectors. The result will be fewer examples of companies getting into trouble and ending up in the wrong part of the business.

WHAT IS BRAND IDENTITY?

Which is the personality of the brand? And how to grow an incredible one.

We will start things off with a definition. What does the term brand identity mean?

Brand identity is the set of all the components a business manufactures to communicate to the customer the right picture. Brand identity differs from "brand image" and "brand," although these terms are sometimes treated as interchangeable.

The term trademark refers to the marketing practice of actively designing a distinctive brand. A brand is the perception of the company in the eyes of the world.

Let's dig a little deeper.

Assume you 're a kid in middle school. As an ambitious kid, you want to be cool and welcome to sit at the coffee shop 's best table. But you can't just use the picture of other men. You have to do some research to grow this brand.

So, make sure to watch the right YouTube channels, so you always know the latest meme. Maybe you will start working on your free throw. And it retains the impression of Mr. Archibald, your science teacher. These actions are the work you put into developing the desired image. You are your brand.

Eventually, you must ensure that you watch the segment. Purchase the latest Nike sneakers that everyone needs to save money. You've got a new style of hair. They try (and join) the basketball team.

These tangible elements - the shoes, the haircut, and team membership - are the brand identity.

You will immediately identify your clients with the brand name. Your audience will equate the name of your company with your product or service. The persona establishes a bond between you and your clients, increases customer satisfaction, and defines how your consumers perceive your brand.

How to develop a strong brand identity
You know who you are

You must know who you are as a brand before deciding which specific elements will make up your brand identity.

Those essential things are who you are as a brand:
- Your mission (what is your "why?")
- Your values (what beliefs drive your business?)
- The personality of your brand (if your brand was a person, what kind of personality would you have?)
- Your unique positioning (how do you differ from the competition?)
- Your brand's voice (how does it talk if your brand was a person)

These elements define your brand. Before starting to build a brand identity, it is important to have a clear understanding of each.

Don't sweat, though you find it tough to figure out who you are. Sometimes a simple brainstorming session is enough to get some clarity about who you are as a brand.

Ask yourself:
- Why did we start this business?

- What are the ideals and values essential to us as an organization?
- How better than anyone else are we doing?
- What makes us so special?
- What if we were in three terms to describe our brand? Why?
- What three words do we want to describe to us with our customers?

This great design notebook can be viewed even from the advisory company PricewaterhouseCoopers. While this workbook is personal brand-oriented, strategies work for any type of business model.

When you have decided who you are as a brand, the time has come to build the persona that takes the company to live and show the most important people: the customers.

Design: the foundation of your brand identity

As your Adidas built your personality brand identity as a middle school top athlete, your design will determine your company's brand identity.

The resources of your corporate design are the tangible elements that determine the perception of your brand. Things like logo, packaging, web design, social media graphics, business cards, and uniforms worn by employees.

In other words: nailing the design = nailing the brand identity = building a successful company that accurately reflects who you are as a brand.

How do you nail your design and build a brand identity that takes your business to the next level?

Develop your brand design

Before you start creating design resources, you need to start over with the basics of the design structure: the building blocks of brand identity.

The building blocks you want to identify before creating the design elements include:

Typography

Typography refers - as you guessed it - to the character (or type) you choose for your brand materials. It is particularly important to choose the logo and brand characters carefully. There are four main types of typography:

- Serif characters (like Times New Roman or Garamond) have an anchor at the end of each letter (or pins for some people). This classic typography is fantastic if you want your brand to appear reliable, traditional, and just a little old-fashioned.
- If "serif" is the foot, "sans serif" is footless. Sans serif characters (like Helvetica or Franklin Gothic) are letters with rounded edges without the anchor or "feet" of their serif counterparts. Sans serif fonts give brands a more elegant and modern look.
- The script typography emulates cursive writing (much for all italic lessons in elementary schools!). These fonts (like Allura or Pacific) can be a great way to give your brand a luxurious or feminine look.
- Display characters are in a separate league. Each display character has a special element, regardless of whether it is an unusual form of

letters, outlines, shadows, or a more artistic / hand-drawn border (think of the Metallica lightning bolt character). Would you like to make a bold declaration and build a brand name that people won't forget? A computer font is an ideal way to do so.

A lot about your brand is the typography you picked. Therefore, wisely pick the fonts.

Color Palette

The color comes next. People, including your potential customers, have psychological ties to different colors. The strategic use of brand colors and logo colors can have a serious impact on how your audience perceives your brand.

Rainbow colors (plus some extras) can support your brand identity as follows:

- Red: The color with love and excitement is red. When the brand name is solid, youthful, and exciting, it is a great choice.

- Orange: orange is another high energy color and is ideal if you want to look friendly and playful. It is used less often than red, so you stand out from the rest.
- Yellow: yellow, the color of the sun, is all, fortunately. The cheerful atmosphere makes it a great choice if you want to feel fun, accessible, and affordable.
- Green: green is an incredibly versatile color and can be used for almost any brand. Culturally, when people see green, they think two things: money or nature. If your brand is tied to one of these things, green is a particularly good choice.
- Blue: blue is the most universally attractive color in the spectrum and can help make your brand more stable and reliable. So if you want to target a large population and make them trust you, choose blue.
- Purple: purple is the color of the royal family. So if you want to have a feeling of luxury in your brand, that's for sure.

- Rosa: right or wrong; pink is culturally linked to femininity. So pink would be a sure candidate for the color of your brand if your company is aimed at women. This is also an outstanding paint for soft or premium products.
- Brown: brown may be the least used color in the overall brand, but it may work to your advantage! Whenever you do something different, you can stand out from the rest. Brown can also help people see your brand as robust or masculine.
- Black: if you want to be considered modern or sophisticated, there is nothing more classic and effective than black.

Form

When it comes to your projects, you also need to think about form and shape. This subtle but effective element, which you can use to reinforce your customers' desired reaction: a logo consisting only of circles and soft edges will produce a completely different reaction than a crisp and square one.

Here is how different shapes can shape your brand identity (pun intended):

- Round shapes - like circles, ovals, and ellipses - relate to heat and blur. Brands with round shapes can create feelings of community, unity, and love. Rounded edges can also be considered feminine.
- Straight lines - such as squares, rectangles, and triangles - cause people to think about strength and efficiency. The no-frills lines create a sense of stability and reliability. Still, you have to be careful: if the shapes are not balanced by something fun, like dynamic colors, they may seem impersonal and not connect with your customers.
- Straight lines also have their effects: vertical lines indicate masculinity and strength, while horizontal lines indicate a calm and gentle mood.

Design your brand identity

Once you've identified the building blocks of your design, it's time to work with a designer to bring your brand identity to life and translate your brand into concrete design resources that you can use in your marketing. The brand identity can be expressed in any number of elements. Depending on the type of company, one or the other resource can be more or less important. For example, a restaurant should think a lot about its menu and physical space. However, a digital marketing agency needs to focus more on its website and social media pages.

The common elements of the brand identity are:
Logo
The logo design is the cornerstone of brand identity. When you work with your designer, you want your logo to tick the following boxes:
- Communicate clearly who you are and what you value as a brand;
- It is visually appealing: simple, clean and clear is a long way;
- It's classic, not trendy: the last thing you want is for your logo to go out of style in 6 months.

- Play with your industry standards - and if you deviate from them, you do it on purpose.
- Makes a lasting impression on your audience.

You will have to ensure that a logo is available in various forms (such as black and white or different sizes) by the design team to ensure that you are always given the logo you need and that any logo suits the brand's branding.

Website

Your website is one of the brand identity's most important elements. For a fact, your clients should certainly check your website if they want to do business with you, whether you are doing a business online or a digital product. It is necessary to represent your brand name entirely on your website.

Product packaging

If your product is a physical product, product packaging is the key to attracting the right customers. Whether you think of the bottle of a cold-brewed drink or the mail you send to your customers who bought clothing from your e-commerce business, don't underestimate the value of good designs to improve the driving experience drive both loyalty and repeated purchases. The packaging is a great opportunity to make your design shine.

Business cards

If you are doing any kind of business development (and who is not), you should stock up on business cards. A well-designed card offers the opportunity to reinforce a positive opinion about you in the eyes of potential customers or clients. When it comes to designing business cards, be simple: your company logo on one side of the card and your most important personal information on the other should suffice.

E-mail design

E-mail is an ideal way to get the customers engaged and support the business. Most workers are overworked, though. And you need the right idea plan to stand out from the chaos if you want to expand your company via e-mail. Think about the purpose of the e-mail. Are you trying to establish a personal connection? So keep it short, sweet, and simple. You're trying to educate. So format it well, so it's easy to read and scan and add some pictures to make it pop. Are you trying to tell your customers a new line of clothing that you have launched? Focus on some extraordinary product images.

Create a brand style guide

Once you have the design resources, you want to make sure they are used correctly. For this reason, you want to create a brand style guide. This document, which describes your design's resources, when and how you use them, as well as all the activities of design and the do for your brand, ensures that each future project corresponds to the identity of your brand and generates the right perception between your audience.

Cohesion is the secret to creating a solid identity for the company. You don't want to make your name look different from your website on social media. This would confuse customers and make your brand less reliable and professional. Therefore, always adhere to a brand guide that covers all the different elements of brand identity. In this way, you can create brand awareness and long-term loyalty.

Brand identity in brief ...

Your brand identity sets you apart from the endless sea of competition and shows your customers who you are and what they can expect to work with you. So if you wish to see the company favorably, you will define the corporate name so concepts that demonstrate your buyers who you are specifically. So it is time to begin planning, now that you know how to understand this name.

CONCLUSION

Virtual sales: the secret of selling to customers

Data and technological advances such as artificial intelligence provide salespeople with a vision of increasing productivity and ROI. With this business acceleration, sellers must introduce new and creative ways to sell to a customer, such as virtual sales.

Despite extensive activities, the sales staff is constantly striving to spend more time with potential customers and current customers. In an age of relentless globalization, the virtual link, which contributes to higher profits, is one of the main improvements made lately.

When virtual sales reach a turning point, customers are less likely to rely on face-to-face meetings.

A recent sales status report found that in Australia and New Zealand over the past three years, 57% of employees have increased their time to virtually contact customers or potential customers (a net change of 6%), while 52 % increased the time they spent personal meetings (with a net change of 4%).

Old versus new world

Building relationships - this is the old world of sales. Personal sales were a prerequisite for success, especially in the B2B context. But now sales are facing a different world.

Sales-enhancing relationships aren't just about the time you spend. They are also based on understanding and supporting the strategic directions of companies. From a virtual point of view, this means the use of other technologies such as Google Hangouts, Skype, or other videoconferencing or telepresence tools.

Nowadays, sellers are often driven to contact as many customers and potential customers as possible. Since customers also require more efficient integration, technology is being used in a completely new way.

"The relationships that increase sales are based not only on the time you spend but also on understanding and supporting the companies' strategic directions."

Customers (and potential customers) are now much better informed than before. They accessed the information and completed due diligence and reference reviews before connecting with potential suppliers.

As a result, buyers get involved when their buying cycle fits, rather than being guided by traditional sales cycles. In this new environment, a sales representative must respond quickly, be relevant, and be as informed as the buyer is.

Technology, including virtual connection to your business, plays an important role in a seller's ability to do these three things.

All about adding value

It is essential to create added value in a good time. Salespeople can use virtual sales to reach multiple customers or even reach customers in different geographic areas. Technology can shorten the sales cycle and allow employees to be "present" to customers when needed.

Here are some strategies that companies should adopt and guide:

- Win the war on attention - Understand that the people in your customer base have different preferences regarding how they want to be communicated and sold at different points in the sales and purchase process. Communicate with them using the virtual tools they want and to get them.
- Data-driven analysis made possible by technology: the availability of comprehensive data and the ability to derive information leads to more effective methods of prioritizing and predicting the leads that promote success.
- Building valuable relationships - With insights based on data being processed by artificial intelligence (AI), employees can easily identify the people and accounts with the greatest propensity to buy, freeing up their time for things that cannot be automated, how to focus on building valuable relationships with the right prospects at the right time.

Virtual sales and changes in staffing patterns

Since sales are virtual, hiring practices reflect this trend. The sales status report found that the number of employees has increased by 7% on average since 2015 and sales staff by 6%.

High-performance sales organizations are 2.3 times more likely to hire more internal employees than the average below average and 2.7 times more likely to hire more sellers.

While sales managers cite several reasons for switching to a human resource model for internal sales, including the best opportunity to specialize agents and reduce costs, the best technology is the main motivator.

"Sales representatives can use virtual sales to reach multiple customers or even reach customers in different geographic areas."

The internal sales role developed outside the appointment for field sales roles, focusing on the customer. It is a method of including sales without being physically present.

Prepare for the future

As customers continue to expect continuous, personalized, and fast experiences at every stage of their journey, companies must dismantle the silos and use a free internal flow of customer data. Cooperation between business areas is becoming more critical.

Therefore, AI quickly became a required item for fast and profitable sales. The new level of knowledge and automation would significantly improve efficiency by simplifying routine or data-based operations, including the concept of lead priorities and results.

With AI-supported virtual sales, employees can quickly access customer information to be relevant to customers. It is not a customer's job to understand the relevance of a representative as a seller. It is a representative's job to be relevant, and technology allows it.

Sales representatives must also be able to rely on technology and AI adoption to strengthen sales teams' role, but not to replace the role of a sales professional. The sales teams who accept it and make the most of them are well-positioned for business success.

Do Not Go Yet; One Last Thing To Do

If you enjoyed this book or found it useful, I'd be very grateful if you'd post a short review on Amazon. Your support does make a difference, and I read all the reviews personally so I can get your feedback and make this book even better.

Thanks for your help again!

Made in the USA
Middletown, DE
15 November 2020